National Audit Office

AF884891

HM Treasury and Cabinet Office

Improving government's planning and spending framework

Report by the Comptroller and Auditor General

Ordered by the House of Commons
to be printed on 26 November 2018

This report has been prepared under Section 6 of the National Audit Act 1983 for presentation to the House of Commons in accordance with Section 9 of the Act

Sir Amyas Morse KCB
Comptroller and Auditor General
National Audit Office

23 November 2018

HC 1679 | £10.00

This report examines the progress made by the Cabinet Office and HM Treasury in improving the government's planning and spending framework since we last reported in 2016.

005048 11/18 NAO

Contents

The National Audit Office study team consisted of:
Jonathan Bayliss, Vicky Davis, Huyen Do, Antonia Gracie, Linh Nguyen, Sarah Perryman, Emma Taylor, under the direction of Siân Jones.

This report can be found on the National Audit Office website at www.nao.org.uk

For further information about the National Audit Office please contact:

National Audit Office
Press Office
157–197 Buckingham Palace Road
Victoria
London
SW1W 9SP

Tel: 020 7798 7400

Enquiries: www.nao.org.uk/contact-us

Website: www.nao.org.uk

Twitter: @NAOorguk

Key facts

2015	£4tn	15
the year single departmental plans were introduced	allocated at Spending Review 2015 for total public spending for the five years to 2020-21	of 17 government departments had an approved 2018-19 single departmental plan by September 2018

Three to five number of years usually covered by allocations at spending reviews

One-fifth HM Treasury staff work in spending teams

24 costing projects carried out to date by HM Treasury and departments to identify and understand cost drivers and potential efficiencies in specific areas of spending

Of the officials involved in business planning and spending who responded to our survey:

92% agreed that HM Treasury spending teams actively seek to build a constructive and transparent relationship with them

75% said that their department's single departmental plan had clear and agreed objectives

53% told us their 2018-19 single departmental plans aligned proposed deliveries with actual capability and capacity

33% agreed that HM Treasury spending teams provided mechanisms to support and encourage departments to work together

Summary

1 The way central government plans and allocates resources is critical to improving the efficiency and effectiveness of public spending. To deliver value for money over the medium to longer term, government needs an integrated planning and spending framework which provides: robust realistic plans, with clear priorities; long-term clarity on funding that supports organisations to work together across government and protect value for money; good understanding of outcomes and monitoring of performance against them in-year; and the ability to identify new priorities and reshape plans systematically in light of events or performance.

2 The roles and responsibilities in central government's planning and spending framework are threefold:

- Departments, led by accounting officers, plan and deliver their objectives and they are accountable for their delegated budgets.
- HM Treasury is responsible for allocating and controlling public spending; scrutinising and approving project and programme spending outside of departments' delegated limits and novel and contentious proposals, with the aim of delivering value for money.[1] It delegates budgets to departments; and sets rules for government financial management. Its 20 spending teams advise HM Treasury ministers on decisions at spending reviews; review and approve submissions for new spending on projects and programmes; and monitor departments' budgets and spending risks.
- The Cabinet Office monitors delivery of departments' objectives and government policy priorities and oversees departmental business planning.

3 In March 2018, the Chancellor announced that HM Treasury would carry out a spending review in 2019. A spending review usually sets spending limits for departments over approximately three to five years, subject to fiscal forecasts. HM Treasury introduced multi-year budgets in 1998, and can grant departments flexibility to move funding between years, which can help with medium-term financial planning and management, as most objectives straddle financial years. Between spending reviews, HM Treasury allocates money including at annual budgets, monitors spending risks, scrutinises value for money of new proposals, and authorises in-year adjustments.

1 HM Treasury, *Managing Public Money*, July 2013 with annexes revised as at March 2018; HM Treasury, *The Green Book - Central government guidance on appraisal and evaluation*, 2018; and, HM Treasury, *Treasury approvals process for programmes and projects*, November 2016.

4 Since 2015, each department has been required to prepare an annual internal business plan, known as a single departmental plan (SDP). It sets out how the department intends to implement its objectives and government manifesto commitments, and deliver public services within its spending limit. The first SDPs did not inform the 2015 Spending Review as they were not finalised until after it was completed.

5 This report reviews government's progress in improving the planning and spending framework since we last reported in July 2016,[2] and the way in which HM Treasury and the Cabinet Office have sought to address the systemic issues around planning and spending decisions that we have identified in our work across government. We set out:

- the current planning and spending framework and the approach to long-term planning (Part One);
- the evolution of medium-term business planning (Part Two);
- the evolution of HM Treasury's approach to managing spending in the short term (Part Three); and
- the challenges for the 2019 Spending Review and beyond (Part Four).

6 We aim to inform the continued development of departmental planning and future spending reviews. Our evaluative criteria and methods are included in Appendices One and Two. Appendix Three sets out the Committee of Public Accounts' previous recommendations and government's responses on this topic.

Key findings

7 In 2016 we found improvements in the way central government handled spending reviews and managed performance. But we highlighted the absence of an overarching strategic framework for achieving government's objectives and balancing short-term priorities with long-term value for money. We urged government to retain and further develop the new SDP regime to improve the rigour of business planning and prioritisation, particularly in light of the challenges of preparing for the UK's exit from the European Union (EU).

2 Comptroller and Auditor General, *Government's management of its performance: progress with single departmental plans*, Session 2016-17, HC 872, National Audit Office, July 2016; Comptroller and Auditor General, *Spending Review 2015*, Session 2016-17, HC 571, National Audit Office, July 2016

8 The way in which spending of taxpayers' money is budgeted, approved by Parliament and allocated by HM Treasury to departments, is well established and effectively controlled. This system has enabled HM Treasury, through its oversight of departments, to keep spending close to forecasts in the short term, and work towards fiscal targets to reduce government borrowing and debt, as reported by the Office for Budget Responsibility. HM Treasury scrutinises the deliverability and value for money of new proposals for projects and programmes, but ongoing monitoring of benefits is more variable. It is now considering how it can better embed the concept of public value into its scrutiny, and commissioned a review from Sir Michael Barber about how government understands and measures the public value that is delivered with public spending.[3,4] The Chief Secretary to the Treasury noted in the review that government needed to track how it turns public money into results for citizens, and prioritise to ensure that resources are allocated to where they will be most effective. HM Treasury has not yet decided how best to implement the findings of the review. At the same time, the Cabinet Office – through SDPs – is helping to improve departments' business planning. The two departments are still working on how these developments will be used in the next Spending Review.

9 We welcome the move towards better understanding and measuring of public value and expect HM Treasury to take this work forward at pace. Following government's commitment to retain and build on the SDP regime, we would urge HM Treasury and the Cabinet Office to work closely together to support government's business planning into the future. In our view, the benefits of bringing these and other improvements together, to create a more integrated planning and spending framework, are self-evident. Such a framework would allow government to adopt a consistent and coherent approach when overseeing the delivery of projects and programmes, with enough checks and balances to ensure correction if things go awry. Without such a framework, there is a real risk that the system is vulnerable to short-term thinking, which often leads to poor outcomes for those relying on public services and jeopardises value for money.

3 HM Treasury, *Delivering better outcomes for citizens: practical steps for unlocking public value*, led by Sir Michael Barber, November 2017.

4 The Barber review defines "public value" as the value created when public money is translated into outputs and outcomes which improve people's lives and economic wellbeing.

10 Our report can help government as it works to put these ideas into practice. In setting out our key findings, we focus on how well integrated business planning and spending management is and the extent to which it supports:

- **achieving long-term value for money:** long-term planning to deliver government policy objectives and sustainable public services; clarity where it is needed about funding beyond the end of the current spending review period; and an understanding of what is being delivered with that funding. To deliver long-term value, plans must be consistent and subject to good policing by HM Treasury, the Cabinet Office and the departments themselves;
- **realistic planning, challenge and prioritisation in the medium term:** robust business plans with clear priorities, linked to the available resources and underpinned by monitoring and reporting on progress and outcomes. HM Treasury spending teams, alongside departments' finance teams, need to defend plans against unrealistic or optimistic assumptions; and
- **short-term spending control and performance management:** a clear view of in-year performance and resource use, and the ability to make changes to plans with an understanding of the impact this will have on medium- and longer-term value for money and without undermining delivery of longer-term goals.

Achieving long-term value for money

11 HM Treasury has begun to focus more on the longer term. The Office for Budget Responsibility now independently assesses fiscal risks alongside its existing role of assessing the long-term sustainability of the public finances, to which HM Treasury responds formally. Established by HM Treasury, the National Infrastructure Commission makes recommendations on long-term infrastructure needs. HM Treasury is providing guaranteed levels of funding in areas such as the NHS – which will receive a real-terms increase over the next five years – to support 10-year planning, and reforming areas of long-term spending such as pensions. It is also increasingly focusing on longer-term fiscal risks through its analysis of the government's balance sheet, which is based on the Whole of Government Accounts and aims to improve management of the government's assets and liabilities (paragraphs 1.14 to 1.19).

12 Yet spending teams' routine monitoring does not focus on long-term risks. We found HM Treasury spending teams' engagement with the balance sheet review varies and this work has yet to make a difference to the way spending teams monitor departments. When monitoring risks for departments, the spending teams are mainly focused on risks to in-year and medium-term budgets rather than long-term risks. Fewer than one-half of departments' finance and planning officials responding to our survey thought that spending teams considered the long-term impact of funding decisions on outcomes. Survey respondents wanted a longer-term view of funding from the centre of government, to support better planning. Departments told us that their attention is directed to staying within budget in the current financial year, rather than the medium or longer term. For example, despite having a 10-year plan since 2012, the Ministry of Defence is still focused on addressing short-term funding gaps. We have reported for a second year that the Equipment Plan is unaffordable. To help close the gap, the Ministry has reduced investment and delayed work programmes, which could increase risks to value for money in the longer-term (paragraphs 1.17, 1.19 and 2.12 and Figures 14, 19 and 22).

13 Long-term funding is not supported by a good understanding of the longer-term value for money of public spending. The removal of Public Service Agreements (PSAs) in 2010 left a vacuum in terms of measuring the long-term performance and value delivered by government spending.[5] Where longer-term funding has been agreed (for example, the housing and NHS settlements), the detailed long-term plans and HM Treasury's role in monitoring delivery are still being developed. HM Treasury's past attempts to improve understanding and management of value have had limited impact and have not been sustained. Following the Barber Review, HM Treasury is now developing an approach to understanding public value which could help inform spending allocations at the 2019 Spending Review. However, the project is at an early stage and HM Treasury is considering how it will make use of the pilot work in future (paragraphs 1.9 to 1.12, 1.19 and Figure 4).

14 HM Treasury's own success measures prioritise spending control over long-term value for money. Spending teams use value for money criteria when scrutinising projects and programmes which exceed departments' delegated limits. Eighty-four per cent of survey respondents agreed that HM Treasury challenges value for money of funding bids. However, spending teams do not routinely monitor departmental performance against an agreed set of objectives. HM Treasury itself has an objective of ensuring value for money and improving outcomes, but the only measures it uses to assess its performance are the reduction in government borrowing and the reduction in government debt. Against these measures, HM Treasury performs strongly, delivering tight spending control. The International Monetary Fund's analysis shows that the UK has been the most successful country in the EU at meeting its spending forecasts in the last 15 years. But the measures can create incentives to favour short-term savings over longer-term value for money – as we have seen in HM Treasury's past decisions on the use of private finance and asset sales (paragraphs 3.4, 3.5, 3.16, 3.18, 4.2 to 4.5 and Figures 18 and 23).

5 In 1998, the then government introduced a framework of PSAs as the primary means to set its key, top priority objectives and measure performance against them. Departments and HM Treasury agreed PSAs as part of the spending review process. In return for funding, departments agreed to deliver key outcomes such as reducing child poverty, tackling climate change and improving healthcare.

Realistic planning, challenge and prioritisation in the medium term

15 **The Cabinet Office is working to make SDPs an enduring basis for improved business planning and spending allocation.** The Cabinet Office has retained and built upon the business planning regime it introduced in 2015, which is based around SDPs. SDPs are intended as comprehensive, costed business plans that departments develop to set out and agree the choices about what must be delivered within their spending limits, manage business and track their performance. The Cabinet Office is working with HM Treasury and the Government Finance Function to support and challenge departments and has asked them to self-assess the maturity of their business planning processes. Other expert cross-government functions are providing support in areas such as project management and contracting (paragraphs 1.7, 2.1, 2.3 to 2.8 and Figures 2 and 7).

16 **SDPs and performance information are not yet central to decision-making in all departments.** Not all departments have aligned their internal decision-making with the SDP they present to the Cabinet Office and HM Treasury. SDPs cannot support better value for money unless they drive day-to-day decisions about how to spend money, and using SDPs for decision-making will help improve their quality. We found that few HM Treasury spending teams we examined refer routinely to SDPs. Together with the Cabinet Office, HM Treasury is working on how to use SDPs to challenge bids and inform allocations at the next Spending Review (paragraphs 2.5, 2.13, 3.14, 3.15 and 4.18).

17 **Departments do not fully integrate delivery planning with financial and workforce planning, and measures of performance and value for money are weak.** Departmental officials in our survey reported improvement against all the key elements of business planning. Departments we spoke to said the SDP approach had helped them clarify objectives and internal accountabilities, and take a more professional approach to planning. However, some departments did not include in their SDPs all the information that was required in the guidance. Some were not able to produce financial and workforce plans for the medium term, or integrate these with the outputs and outcomes they propose to deliver. Departments are still weak on setting out their understanding of the relationship between inputs, outputs and outcomes, and making use of performance data for decision-making. This creates a risk of making unachievable commitments and failing to see when they are off-track (paragraphs 2.1, 2.6, 2.7, 2.10 and 2.11, Figures 9 and 10).

18 Over-optimism and unwillingness to prioritise are entrenched problems. With rising demands and fixed spending limits, departments have had to plan to deliver more with less. Several departments are also attempting to steer complex, long-term programmes of transformation in public services. Moving services online, for example, can offer large efficiency savings in the longer term, but these may fail to materialise without realistic planning and management. Our work shows repeatedly how over-optimistic plans for delivery or savings (such as the efficiency targets set for hospitals) are followed by either failure to deliver, lower service quality, or a need for later funding injections. At the root of this problem lies not only poor data on costs and performance, but also inconsistent challenge, both within departments and by the centre of government. Only one-half of survey respondents told us the proposed deliveries in their SDPs matched actual capability and capacity. Staff involved in business planning say they find it difficult to say no to new ministerial priorities. And while we found examples of departments making tactical adjustments to their programmes to meet the immediate pressures of EU Exit work, there was little sign of strategic reprioritisation or activities being dropped. The Cabinet Office and HM Treasury could do more to use SDPs to challenge departments' costings, and to examine overall affordability, deliverability and risk in government's combined plans (paragraphs 2.6, 2.13 to 2.17, 3.14, 3.15, 4.7 and 4.18 and Figures 6, 15, 16, 17 and 19).

19 Business planning does not help to break down government silos. Many government objectives, from overseas aid to children's mental health services, cut across multiple departments and public bodies. The guidance to departments on SDPs requires them to report on contributions to cross-government objectives. But government's structure of departments, with separate accountabilities, leads to business planning and spending review submissions being created in silos. This can undermine overall value for money, and negatively affect local services, because multiple central government departments take separate, narrow views. Government told us that seven Cabinet-level implementation taskforces and a number of HM Treasury groups are working on various cross-government risks and priorities, including housing, modern slavery and the ageing society. But none of these publish plans and there is no visibility of their impact. HM Treasury considers that its costing projects have helped improve understanding of activities that cut across government and encouraged collaboration – but these are in selected areas only. HM Treasury told us that it is trying to encourage cross-departmental bids and will consider how best to allow for this in the next Spending Review (paragraphs 3.14, 4.8 to 4.11 and Figure 24).

20 **There is a demand for greater transparency, both within and outside government, over the basis for spending choices.** Spending reviews have previously been characterised by a bilateral deal-making approach between departments and HM Treasury, and a lack of collaboration between departments – this is consistent with an emphasis on controlling individual budgets, but does not encourage a joined-up approach to value for money. SDPs are not formally shared between departments. Departments told us they would like HM Treasury to have open conversations about the spending review process, align it with government's high-level strategic objectives, and incorporate checks to stop 'problem-shifting' between departments (for example the impact of welfare reforms on the increase in homelessness, which had not been fully assessed when we reported in 2017). HM Treasury is discussing planning for the next Spending Review with senior finance staff in departments. Parliament has also made clear that it wants greater visibility of government's spending choices, but traditionally only details of the outcomes have been published, whereas details of how decisions are reached have not (paragraphs 1.6, 4.10, 4.13, 4.16 and 4.17 and Figure 24).

Short-term spending control and performance management

21 **Over-optimistic plans which are not aligned to resources create in-year spending pressures and put value for money at risk.** Accounting officers are required to plan on an affordable and sustainable path, within their agreed spending limits and in a way that delivers good value for the Exchequer as a whole.[6] However, there are weak incentives to prioritise, make realistic plans and consider longer-term value. We have highlighted previously the effects on local government and health sectors, which have come to rely on using capital funding to pay for day-to-day activities. The Committee of Public Accounts concluded in April 2018 that the system for funding and financially supporting the NHS focuses too much on short-term survival, and that cash injections paper over the cracks in finances rather than achieve lasting improvement (paragraphs 3.6, 4.3, 4.12 and 4.13 and Figures 6 and 19).

22 **HM Treasury spending teams have good relationships with departments.** The quality of the dialogue between departments and HM Treasury spending teams is crucial, as they provide the day-to-day challenge and support to departments' spending. More than 90% of survey respondents agreed that spending teams actively seek to build a constructive and transparent relationship with them. HM Treasury agreed in 2016 that its spending teams should focus more on information about departments' performance, as well as their spending against budget. Spending teams now have access to support from project management and commercial experts in the government functions, as well as insights from HM Treasury's costing projects and value pilots (paragraphs 1.10 to 1.11, 3.2 to 3.4, 3.7, 3.13 to 3.15 and Figure 20).

6 HM Treasury, *Managing Public Money*, Published July 2013, with annexes revised March 2018.

23 **To deliver a more integrated planning and spending framework which prioritises value for money, HM Treasury will require different skills and more capacity from its spending teams.** Departments rated spending teams' skills and capability most highly on policy and analysis, and least on operational delivery experience. HM Treasury highlights influencing skills as important for staff on spending teams. We found a high proportion of these staff are junior. The median time that these staff had been in their current post was eleven months, although HM Treasury data show that the median time they had been working in HM Treasury was just over two years and in the civil service was just over three years.[7] Yet spending teams can lack operational experience, and an ability to understand the issues facing departments and to provide pragmatic solutions. For example, few spending teams we examined refer routinely to departments' SDPs when assessing performance or making spending decisions. The 2018 Budget announcement stated that the 2019 Spending Review will aim to ensure performance and outcomes are tracked systematically, which means an understanding of planning and performance needs to be more central to spending teams' decision-making (paragraphs 3.9 to 3.11, 3.14, 3.15, 4.15 and Figure 21).

Conclusion

24 HM Treasury has, these many years, demonstrated that it is highly effective at controlling public spending. It has, relatively recently, turned its focus towards a renewed drive to improve value for money. There have been positive developments in this direction, not least the Barber review, the provision of specialist advisers to the spending teams and more. Likewise, the Cabinet Office has been working to improve the maturity of business planning across departments.

25 However, there are occasions when we see value for money being compromised by the needs of short-term spending control. Unrealistic, over-optimistic budgets are kept within the spending envelope by short-term unplanned cuts, which can damage long-term programmes and drive suppliers to distraction.

26 All this turbulence can only be minimised by integrated medium- and short-term planning activity, strongly policed and challenged for realism and deliverability by the HM Treasury spending teams, and supported by the Cabinet Office and the civil service functions. This may require different skills and a significant change in mind-set both at the centre of government and in departments. Without these changes, government will continue to be trapped in a cycle of short-termism, over-optimism and silo decision-making, which creates real risks to value for money.

7 As at March 2018.

Recommendations

On integrating planning and spending to deliver long-term value for money for taxpayers

27 HM Treasury should:

a Reflect its commitment to deliver longer-term value for money more strongly in its systems and processes, including performance management of its teams and staff, and arrangements for monitoring departmental performance and risks.

28 HM Treasury and the Cabinet Office should:

b Develop a joint approach to share with departments, explaining how they will bring together information on costs, cross-government objectives, public value, the balance sheet, performance and risk, to challenge departments' bids, and identify joint funding opportunities. Alongside this, HM Treasury should set out how this will inform allocation decisions at the Spending Review, and establish how spending teams will routinely use this information between spending reviews to scrutinise and challenge departments' projects, programmes and performance.

29 The Cabinet Office, working with the functions and HM Treasury, should:

c Based on its review of departments' SDPs and explicit consideration of affordability, capability and risk, create an aggregate understanding of what government can deliver, and how this contributes to its long-term objectives. It should share this with HM Treasury to inform funding allocation decisions.

30 Departments should:

d Demonstrate how they have worked with other departments to consider joint bids where objectives are shared.

On realistic medium-term planning and prioritisation by departments

31 HM Treasury and the Cabinet Office should:

e Make explicit that accounting officers are accountable for producing medium-term business plans that are deliverable – within their expected capability and resource levels – as part of their general accountability for taxpayers' money under *Managing Public Money*.

32 Accounting officers should:

f Provide positive assurance that the medium-term plans they propose are:

- affordable and can be delivered within expected capability; and
- designed to provide value for money for the Exchequer as a whole, having drawn on related activities or objectives in other departments, and on the expertise of the whole civil service, including the functions and non-executive directors.

33 Departments should:

g Use the results of their business planning maturity self-assessment to agree an improvement plan that integrates strategy, finance and workforce planning, and aligns these with the cross-government SDP process, by the beginning of the 2020-21 business planning round.

Part One

Government's planning and spending framework

1.1 The government sets priorities, plans activity, allocates money and monitors its progress and performance using a set of processes that have developed over time.[8] Together, these systems and processes are the planning and spending 'framework'. In 2016, while recognising that there had been improvements, we concluded that government needed a much more integrated framework for planning and managing public sector activity into the medium term and beyond. This framework would be stable and enduring, allowing any government to make achievable plans to deliver its objectives, monitor performance and to adjust as needed to stay on track (**Figure 1**).[9]

1.2 This part examines:

- the roles, responsibilities and activities of the central departments in business planning and managing spending;
- the spending framework;
- the business planning and performance monitoring framework;
- improvement initiatives and the move to a functional model of government; and
- the need for longer-term planning.

Roles, responsibilities and activities of the central departments in business planning and managing spending

1.3 HM Treasury is the government's economics and finance ministry, with overall responsibility for public spending. It has overall responsibility, and sets the rules, for the administration of public money, and delegates funding to accounting officers who lead spending departments. The Cabinet Office supports and monitors the implementation of government's policies and the Prime Minister's priorities. Together, they form the equivalent of a corporate headquarters for government and have complementary roles and responsibilities for business planning, allocating funds and monitoring performance (**Figure 2** on pages 18 and 19).

8 Cabinet Office and HM Treasury, *Guidance: The government's planning and performance framework*, December 2017, available at: www.gov.uk/government/publications/planning-and-performance-framework/the-governments-planning-and-performance-framework

9 Comptroller and Auditor General, *Government's management of its performance: progress with single departmental plans*, Session 2016-17, HC 872; National Audit Office, July 2016; Comptroller and Auditor General, *Spending Review 2015*, Session 2016-17, HC 571, National Audit Office, July 2016.

Figure 1

Pre-requisites for an effective planning and spending framework

Long-term strategic planning (>5 years)

Medium-term business planning (3–5 years)

Short-term budget and performance management (Annual and in-year)

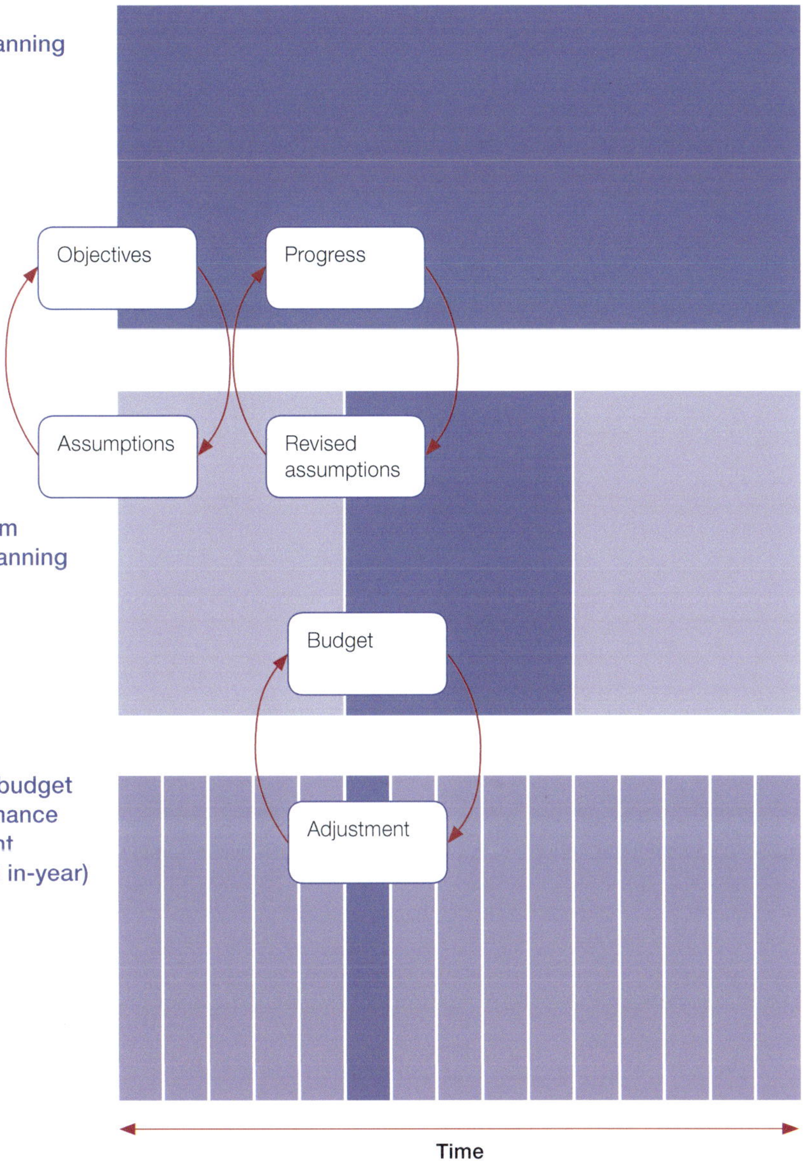

Long-term strategic planning

- Long-term clarity on funding, to support sustainable cross-government working and protect value.
- Clarity on desired long-term outcomes.
- An understanding of high-level objectives and their relative priority.

Medium-term business planning

- Multi-year allocations of funding.
- Robust realistic plans integrated with resources.
- Clear priorities.
- Milestones and medium-term outcome measures.
- Performance metrics.

Short-term budget and performance management

- Annual budget.
- Performance goals.
- In-year monitoring.
- Ability to make adjustments to stay on track.

Source: National Audit Office

The spending framework

1.4 The way taxpayers' money is voted by Parliament to government, allocated by HM Treasury to departments, spent, accounted for and scrutinised, is well established (**Figure 3** on pages 20 and 21). Since 2010, HM Treasury has carried out a spending review every three to five years. The intention of spending reviews is to provide more certainty for departments and the public sector to plan ahead.[10]

10 Cabinet Office and HM Treasury, *Guidance: The government's planning and performance framework*, December 2017.

Figure 2

The parts of central government involved in business planning and spending: examples of activities and interactions with departments

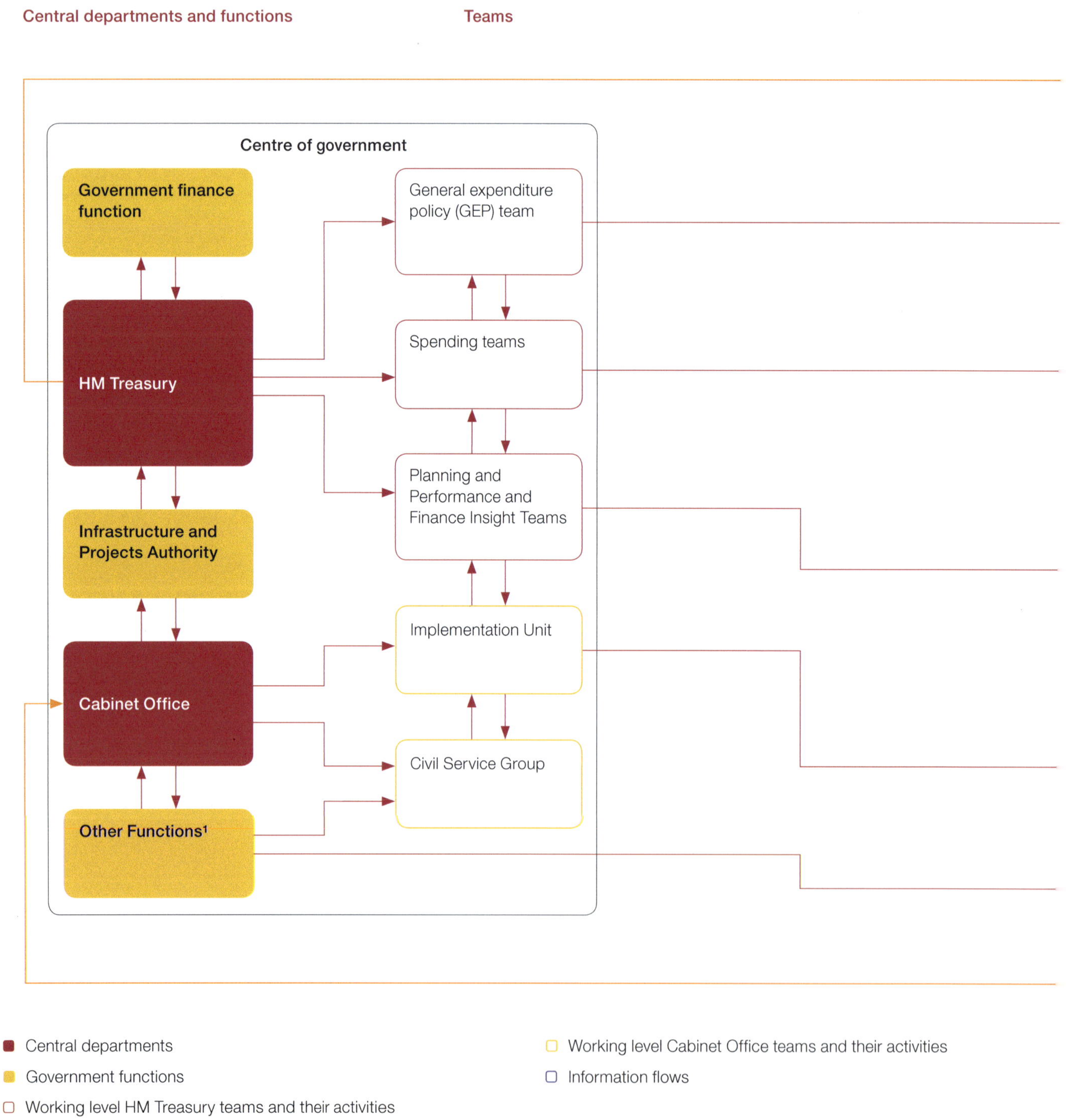

Note

1 See Figure 5 for more detail.

Source: National Audit Office

Activities, interactions and information flows

Pass information to HM Treasury: spending data via OSCAR (online system for central accounting and reporting); forecasts; project business cases; and performance data to spending teams.

Spending analysis e.g. lead spending analysis, model spending review scenarios and keep tally of savings options.

Strategy, negotiations and planning e.g. oversee planning, coordination and governance of spending review, advise ministers on spending review strategy and negotiations, cascade information from ministers and programme board to spending teams.

In-year spending and economics e.g. track delivery of spending review settlements, monitor overall spending risks, oversee GEP's contact with spending teams, and maintain HM Treasury's *Green Book*.

Allocating money e.g. advise on: deliverable spending review settlements; allocations at fiscal events and in-year; and reserve claims.

Controlling spend e.g. forecast spend and monitor and control spending risks.

Set departmental spending conditions with the aim of meeting value-for-money criteria and advise on programme approvals through business cases.

Wider economic policy e.g. scrutinise and advise on policy and how it meets economic goals.

Planning and performance – helping the integration of financial and business planning.

Insight – improving understanding of value for money and what government gets for its money.

Works with the Implementation Unit to support departments in the **production of single departmental plans (SDPs)**.

Aims to **improve and enhance the quality of data and management information** in HM Treasury, functions and departments.

Understanding costs in cross-cutting areas of government work.

Supports departments in the **production of single departmental plans**.

Monitors and supports **delivery of policies within SDPs**.

Advises the PM and Cabinet on progress in implementing SDPs.

Oversees implementation across government and **provides informed advice** on specific implementation issues.

Supports departmental capability.

Bring together specialists within and across departments; work to strengthen capability; deliver expert advice and specialist services.

Civil Service Group coordinates the input of functions to SDPs.

Pass information to the Cabinet Office: quarterly reports on the objectives and work areas in their SDP; and monthly reporting on priority areas agreed with the Cabinet Office and HM Treasury.

Other government departments

Figure 3

Government's planning, spending, monitoring and reporting framework

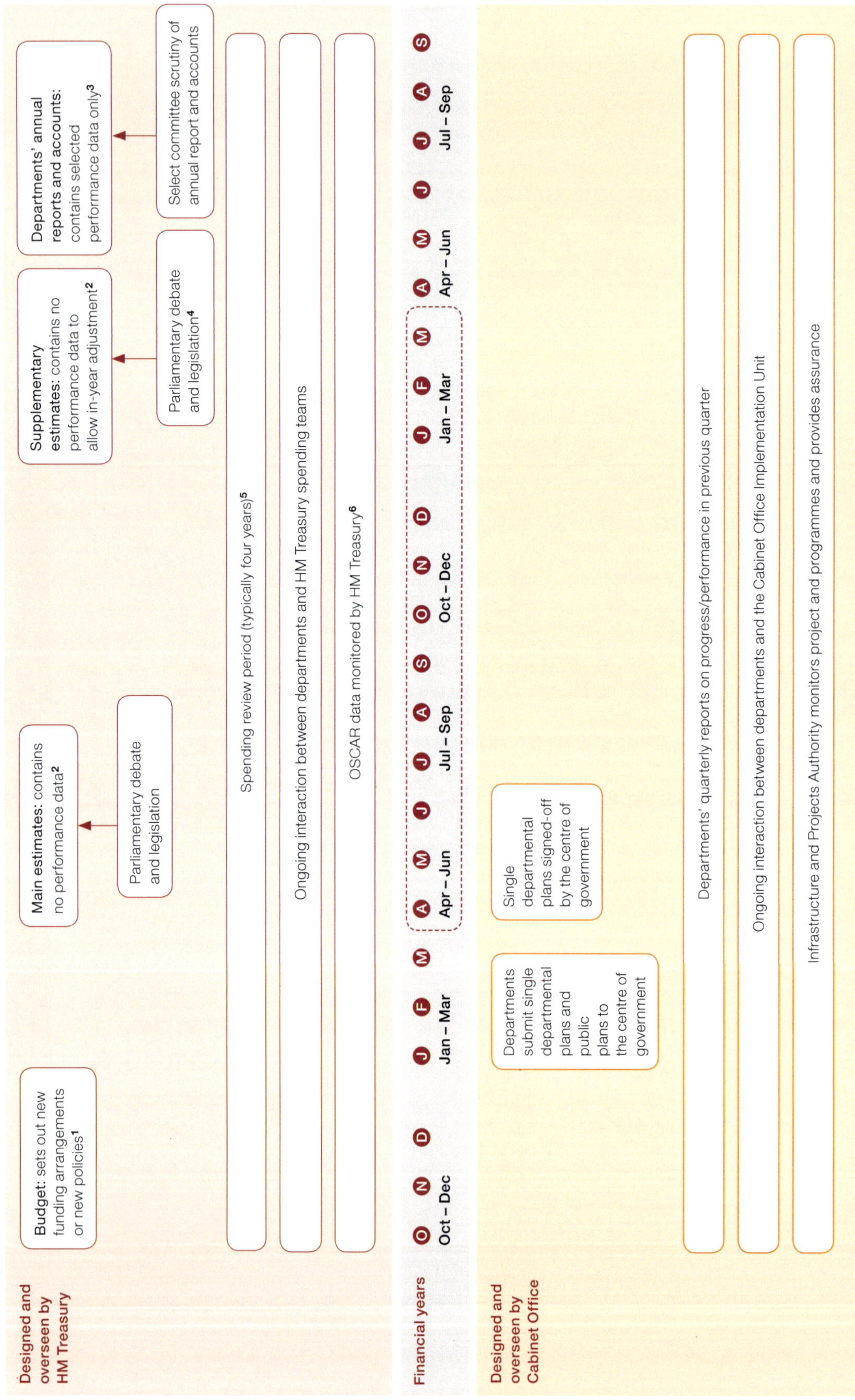

continued

Figure 3 *continued*
Government's planning, spending, monitoring and reporting framework

Notes

1 The Budget also allows for adjustment to previous spending review settlements. Since 2017 the Autumn Budget is the single annual fiscal event, with a Spring Statement providing updates only, not new announcements.

2 Estimates are the means of obtaining from Parliament the legal authority to consume resources and spend cash the government needs to finance departments' agreed spending programmes. Supplementary Estimates are used to seek additional resources, capital and/or cash, or to reallocate existing resources and capital to new activities.

3 2017-18 was the first year of reporting against the objectives set out in single departmental plans (SDPs).

4 In 2016 the Committee of Public Accounts, Public Administration and Constitutional Affairs Committee and House of Commons Procedure Committee all noted that there was no specific Parliamentary scrutiny of budgets, spending reviews or allocative decisions and made relevant recommendations. See, respectively: Appendix 3 of this report; Public Administration and Constitutional Affairs Committee, *Accounting for democracy: making sure Parliament, the people and ministers know how and why public money is spent*, Session 2016-17, HC 95, April 2017; House of Commons Procedure Committee, *Authorising Government expenditure: steps to more effective scrutiny*, Session 2016-17 HC 190, March 2017.

5 In 1998, HM Treasury introduced a new system of public expenditure control. This incorporated a new public expenditure total, a greater distinction between current and capital expenditure, firm multi-year spending limits and increased end-year flexibility.

6 OSCAR is a cross-government public spending database used by HM Treasury to record, monitor and control departments' spending.

Source: National Audit Office

1.5 At a spending review, the overall level of funding is set by reference to forecasts from the independent Office for Budget Responsibility (OBR), and adjusted for any subsequent policy decisions on taxes or borrowing. Within this overall spending envelope, HM Treasury allocates between departments and usually agrees with each its spending limits for the next three to five years. Between spending reviews, HM Treasury may adjust departmental funding including at the annual Budget, making any necessary changes based on new priorities and the latest set of forecasts. Funding is approved, and further adjustments may be made, during the twice-yearly Parliamentary Estimates process (Figure 3).

1.6 The Spending Review 2015 allocated £4 trillion of total public spending for the five years to 2020-21. The next Spending Review is expected in 2019. HM Treasury is discussing planning for the next Spending Review with senior finance staff in departments.

The business planning and performance monitoring framework

1.7 The way government plans, monitors and reports what it has delivered with its funding is not prescribed in legislation. In 2015, government announced a new approach to business planning and performance management, based on single departmental plans (SDPs). SDPs are intended to be comprehensive, costed business plans, bringing together a department's activities and spending in a multi-year plan, which is refreshed annually.[11] Government has said that each department's SDP should act as its internal business plan, setting out how it plans to implement its agreed public commitments, and deliver and transform public services within its spending review settlement. Each is required to include:

- **medium-term financial planning**, covering all years of their departmental spending review settlement and all spending;
- **departmental objectives and activity**: identifying strategic objectives, sub-objectives and work areas;
- **performance indicators**: indicators, resource allocations, milestones/deliverables, key risks and dependencies at each level of objective/activity; and
- **functional statements**: setting out how functions, such as property, digital or commercial, will support the department's activity.

1.8 There is also a public plan for each department, which contains summary information on objectives and activities.[12] For the first time, departments were required to report on performance against SDP objectives in their 2017-18 published annual reports (Figure 3).[13]

Government's improvement initiatives

1.9 Both HM Treasury and Cabinet Office have led initiatives to improve aspects of the efficiency and effectiveness of public spending, but these have not added up to a sustained programme of improvement, and the Committee of Public Accounts has been frustrated by the slow progress (**Figure 4** on pages 24 and 25).[14]

11 Chief Executive of the Civil Service and Permanent Secretary for the Cabinet Office, *Clarifying our priorities – Single Departmental Plans*, July 2015, available at: https://civilservice.blog.gov.uk/2015/07/29/clarifying-our-priorities-single-departmental-plans/; Comptroller and Auditor General, *Government's management of its performance: progress with single departmental plans*, Session 2016-17, HC 872, National Audit Office, July 2016.

12 Cabinet Office, *Building a country that works for everyone: the government's plan*, December 2017, available at: www.gov.uk/government/collections/a-country-that-works-for-everyone-the-governments-plan

13 We have not reviewed departments' reporting of their performance in the 2017-18 annual reports and accounts as part of this work.

14 HC Committee of Public Accounts, *Managing government spending and performance*, Twenty-seventh Report of Session 2016-17, HC 710, November 2016.

1.10 In 2013, HM Treasury's Financial Management Review established initiatives to improve understanding of spending and what has been delivered, but the work done was not used to inform the 2015 Spending Review because it was not detailed enough and not completed consistently across departments.[15,16] Some elements of the work have continued, although they may not be sufficiently advanced to support the 2019 Spending Review.

- **Understanding of costing:** Since 2015, HM Treasury has led 24 projects to identify and understand cost drivers and potential efficiencies in areas of spending ranging from health to justice. HM Treasury plans further costing projects in the run-up to the 2019 Spending Review.
- **Understanding the value from service delivery:** In early 2016, HM Treasury asked departments to create 'value maps', to demonstrate the value delivered and scope for efficiencies in certain key areas of spending. HM Treasury discontinued this work because the self-reporting approach meant it was too subjective, and departments were not always open about the gaps in their understanding.

1.11 In November 2017, HM Treasury published *Delivering better outcomes for citizens: practical steps for unlocking public value*, a report it had commissioned from Sir Michael Barber (the Barber Review).[17] In the preface to the report, the Chief Secretary to the Treasury recognised a need to track how public money is turned into results for citizens; understand the impact of each pound spent; and prioritise to ensure that resources are allocated to where they will be most effective. The Barber Review recommended a 'Public Value' Framework to improve policy outcomes for citizens and measure the likelihood that public spending will produce results that improve people's lives.[18] HM Treasury has been developing and piloting the Framework. As of September 2018, three departments had participated in pilots on a voluntary basis. HM Treasury is considering how best to engage departments with the Framework in future.

15 The Financial Management Review looked at the evolution of HM Treasury's role in spending control and financial management within the history of increasing public accountability for how taxpayers' money is spent and set out how the framework operated in 2013. HM Treasury, *Strengthening financial management capability in government*, June 2013, available at: https://assets.publishing.service.gov.uk/government/uploads/system/uploads/attachment_data/file/209220/strengthening_financial_management_capability_in_government.pdf

16 Comptroller and Auditor General, *Spending Review 2015*, Session 2016-17, HC 571, National Audit Office, July 2016.

17 HM Treasury, *Delivering better outcomes for citizens: practical steps for unlocking public value*, led by Sir Michael Barber, November 2017.

18 The Barber review defines "public value" as the value created when public money is translated into outputs and outcomes which improve people's lives and economic wellbeing.

Figure 4

Timeline of the centre of government's improvement initiatives since 2010

HM Treasury and Cabinet Office have led initiatives to improve aspects of the efficiency and effectiveness of public spending, but these have not added up to a sustained and comprehensive programme of improvement

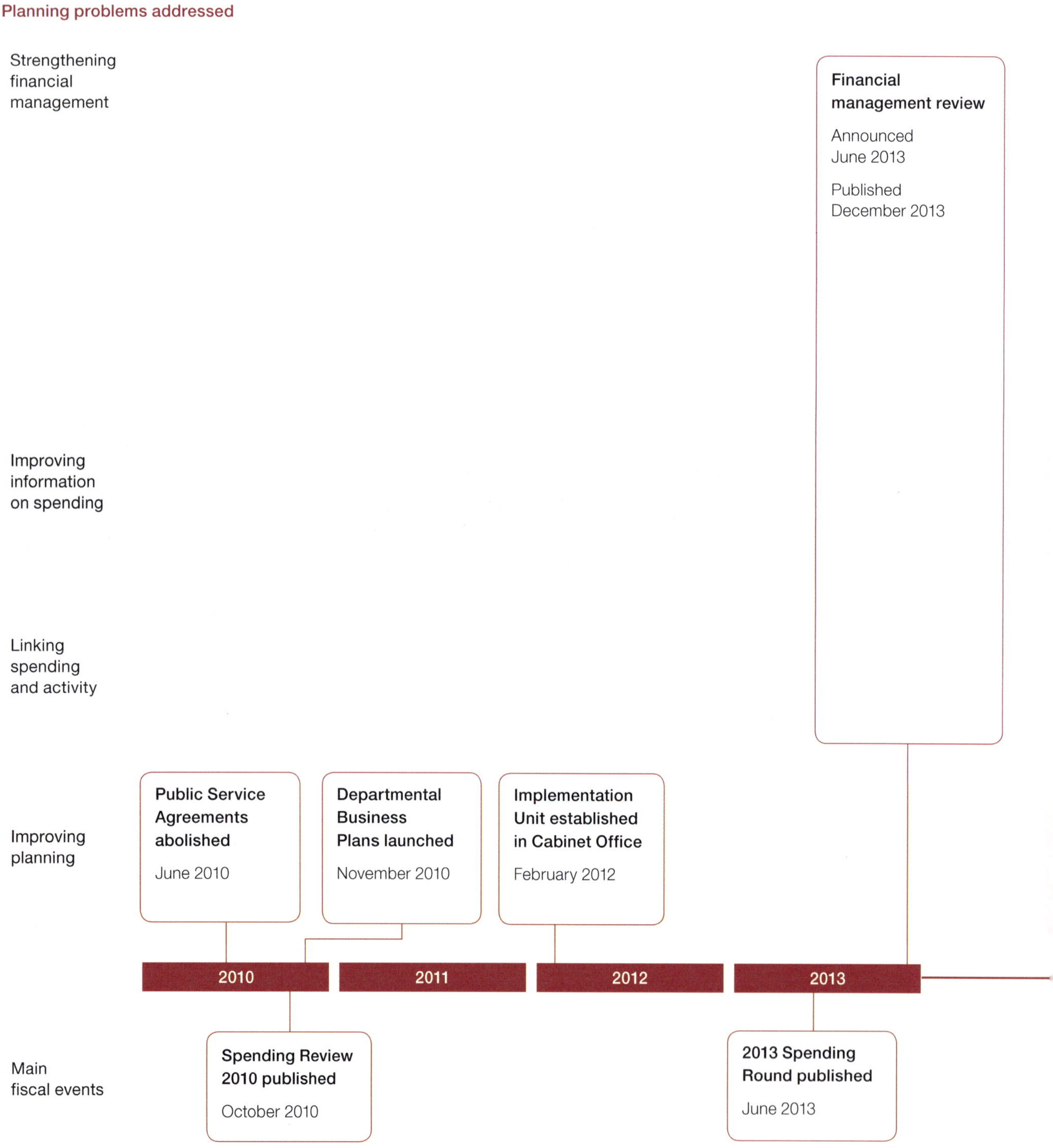

Source: National Audit Office

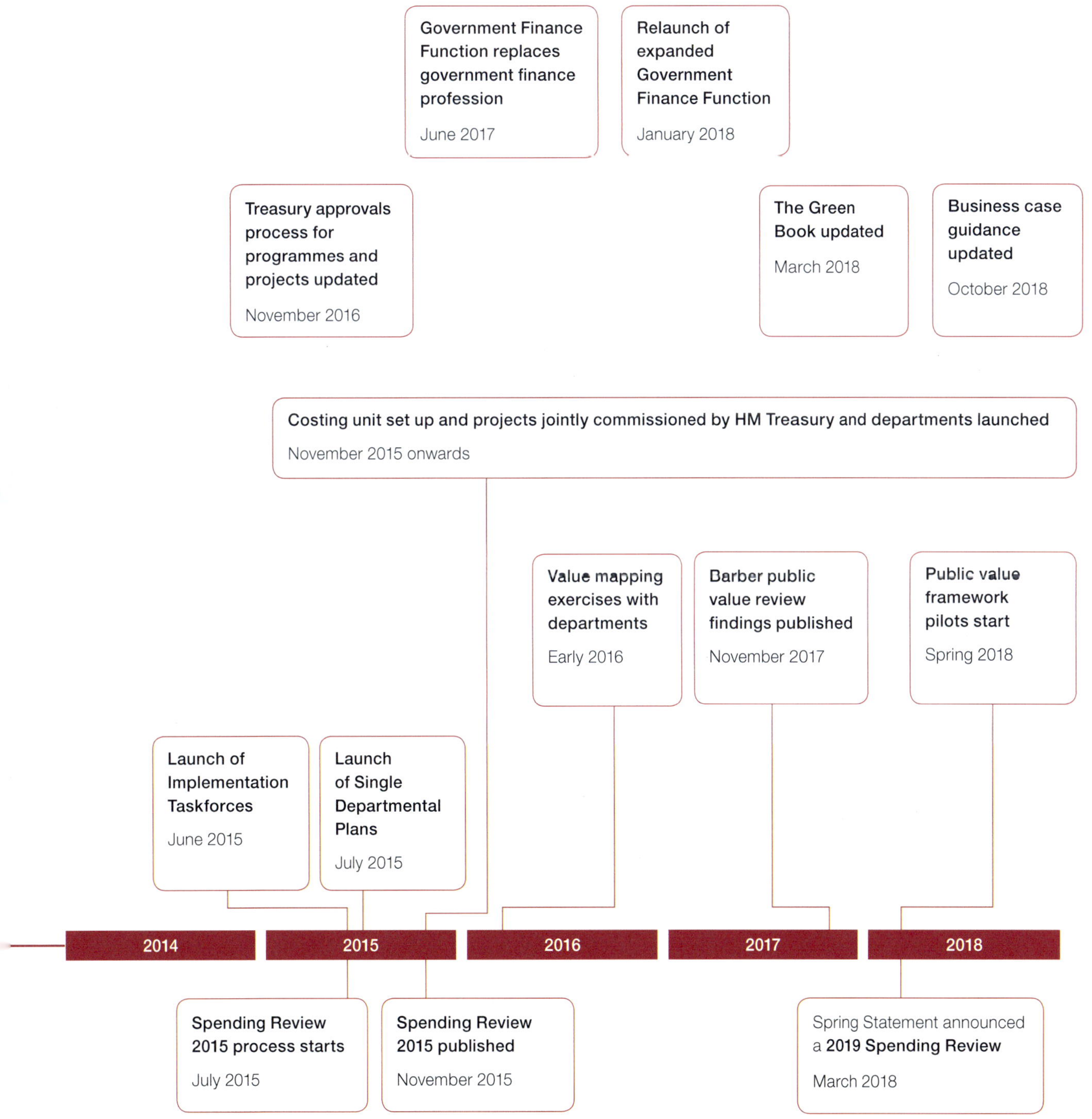
Government Finance Function replaces government finance profession
June 2017
Relaunch of expanded Government Finance Function
January 2018
Treasury approvals process for programmes and projects updated
November 2016
The Green Book updated
March 2018
Business case guidance updated
October 2018
Costing unit set up and projects jointly commissioned by HM Treasury and departments launched
November 2015 onwards
Value mapping exercises with departments
Early 2016
Barber public value review findings published
November 2017
Public value framework pilots start
Spring 2018
Launch of Implementation Taskforces
June 2015
Launch of Single Departmental Plans
July 2015
2014
2015
2016
2017
2018
Spending Review 2015 process starts
July 2015
Spending Review 2015 published
November 2015
Spring Statement announced a 2019 Spending Review
March 2018

1.12 In 2016, we reported on the history of changing arrangements for business planning and performance measurement in government. The move away from Public Service Agreements (PSAs) in 2010 left a vacuum in terms of measuring the long-term performance and outcomes delivered by government spending.[19] Between 2010 and 2015, the centre of government focused on monitoring spending and the cost-efficiency of government back-office activities. From 2012, the Cabinet Office began to take a closer interest in performance again. It created the Implementation Unit, and Cabinet-level Implementation Taskforces to facilitate discussion about priorities that cut across government. From 2015, it developed SDPs and asked departments to start measuring outcomes once again.[20]

The functional model of government

1.13 Since 2015, the civil service has been moving towards a 'functional model'. There is central leadership of 12 cross-departmental corporate functions – such as finance, project delivery and human resources – that aim to develop capability, give expert advice, set and assure standards, set cross-government strategies and drive improvement (**Figure 5**).[21] The functions are at varying degrees of maturity and their operating and accountability models are still developing.

The need for longer-term planning in government

1.14 In October 2016 the Committee of Public Accounts concluded: "departments still focus on the current financial year and longer-term plans are often lacking in detail. Yet many projects and programmes are long-term and multi-faceted and need more sophisticated management."[22] The absence of long-term plans can adversely affect value for money (**Figure 6** on page 28).

Understanding and managing longer-term risks

1.15 Since 2016, HM Treasury has made progress in understanding and managing longer-term risks at the overall fiscal level. It expanded the OBR's role to encompass comprehensive analysis of fiscal risks on the balance sheet alongside its existing role of assessing the long-term sustainability of the public finances. OBR published the first-ever independent analysis of this kind in 2017. In its formal response to the OBR analysis, HM Treasury set out the government's strategies for managing these risks and responsibilities for managing them.

19 In 1998, the then Government introduced a framework of PSAs as the primary means to set its top priority objectives and measure performance against them. Departments and HM Treasury agreed PSAs as part of the spending review process. In return for funding, departments agreed to deliver key outcomes such as reducing child poverty, tackling climate change and improving healthcare.

20 Comptroller and Auditor General, *Government's management of its performance: progress with single departmental plans*, Session 2016-17, HC 872, National Audit Office, July 2016.

21 Cabinet Office, *The functional model: a model for more efficient and effective government*, policy paper, March 2015.

22 HC Committee of Public Accounts, *The Government Balance Sheet*, Nineteenth Report of Session 2016-17, HC 485, October 2016.

Figure 5
The government functions

Finance

The Head of the Government Finance Function was appointed in June 2017 and is also the Chief Financial Officer for the Ministry of Justice. The Government Finance Function is an integral part of HM Treasury and works across government. The Function has outlined six strategic priorities to support its ambition to "put finance at the heart of decision making, driving the agenda and not just keeping score."

1 Getting the basics right
Good forecasting, accurate reporting, robust data, efficient transaction processing.

2 People and capability
A high-performing and diverse function, with great people in the right roles with the right skills.

3 Operating model
A modern collaborative finance function that delivers quality services more effectively and efficiently.

4 Finance insight
An informed function with a clear understanding of what we get for our money, using insight to drive value for money.

5 Trusted adviser
The 'go-to' adviser to colleagues to provide expert advice and inform decision-making.

6 Planning and performance
Driving a strong culture of planning and performance, integrating financial planning with business decisions.

Digital

Supporting more effective and efficient delivery of services through common cross-government digital platforms and common technology services for civil servants.

Project delivery

Delivered through the Infrastructure and Projects Authority, it oversees and manages the Government's Major Projects Portfolio and provides assurance and expertise to support and improve the delivery of major projects.

Commercial

Supports government with commercial guidance, procurement advice, market intelligence, and supplier negotiations. Through the Crown Commercial Service, it also acts as a single customer for government in the central procurement of common goods and services.

Civil Service human resources

Provides a source of expertise to departments and professions on all HR issues, including recruitment and strategic workforce planning. It also manages the recruitment process for some departments.

Analysis

Across the function professionals use specialist tools and techniques to gather qualitative and quantitative research, evidence and data to help make better decisions in policy, operations or deliver value for money.

Other functions

Communications; Fraud, error, debt and grants; Internal Audit; Legal; Property; and Security.

Source: National Audit Office analysis

Figure 6

Absence of long-term plans: examples

Report	Findings on long-term planning
Financial sustainability of local authorities 2018, March 2018[1]	The government has announced multiple short-term funding initiatives in recent years and does not have a long-term funding plan for local authorities. Funding has been characterised by multiple, one-off and short-term funding streams and initiatives. Authorities have responded by treating capital receipts as revenue income, and relying on reserves to balance their books.
Sustainability and transformation in the NHS, January 2018[2]	The NHS achieved its overall surplus in 2016-17 by planning a series of measures to rebalance its finances, some of which have restricted the money available for longer-term transformation. For instance, the Department of Health & Social Care transferred funding for capital projects to fund the day-to-day activities of NHS bodies.
Developing new care models through NHS vanguards, June 2018[3]	There was no national plan against which the progress and success of the national [vanguard] programme could be measured, and against which national bodies could be held accountable. In particular, there was no business case, no clear statement of intended objectives and outcomes, and no plan covering the full duration of the programme. While a certain level of flexibility is required in managing a complex programme, the lack of an overall plan can make it harder for organisations involved to strike the right balance between working towards their long-term vision and tackling their immediate priorities.
Ensuring sufficient skilled military personnel, April 2018[4]	[Ministry of Defence] Head Office has not undertaken a longer-term, strategic analysis of the trades with shortfalls or its ability to meet the changing demands for new skills. It has not assessed whether its existing workforce management policies enable it to develop the capabilities that are needed in trades where the demand for new skills is growing, or where shortfalls have endured.
Improving children and young people's mental health services, October 2018[5]	The government has not set out and costed what it must do to achieve its vision for children and young people's mental health services. Current programmes will not deliver the government's proposals in full. It does not have explicit objectives for some proposals, particularly those related to vulnerable groups. The government has not yet identified what actions and budget it will need, what progress it has made so far, and what further work is required.

Notes

1 Comptroller and Auditor General, *Financial sustainability of local authorities 2018*, Session 2017–2019, HC 834, National Audit Office, March 2018.

2 Comptroller and Auditor General, *Sustainability and transformation in the NHS*, Session 2017–2019, HC 719, National Audit Office, January 2018.

3 Comptroller and Auditor General, *Developing new care models through NHS vanguards*, Session 2017–2019, HC 1129, National Audit Office, June 2018.

4 Comptroller and Auditor General, *Ensuring sufficient skilled military personnel*, Session 2017–2019, HC 947, National Audit Office, April 2018.

5 Comptroller and Auditor General, *Improving children and young people's mental health services*, Session 2017–2019, HC 1618, National Audit Office, October 2018.

Source: National Audit Office

1.16 The government balance sheet (the financial statement of what government owns and owes) provides important insight into long-term risks to public finances. HM Treasury has improved its understanding and analysis of the government's balance sheet in response to recommendations from the Committee of Public Accounts, the International Monetary Fund and the National Audit Office.[23] In the 2017 Budget, HM Treasury announced a review of government departments' balance sheet management, which draws on the Whole of Government Accounts and is intended to improve the return on assets and reduce the cost of liabilities. HM Treasury will publish the conclusions from the review at Spending Review 2019.[24]

1.17 As part of HM Treasury's balance sheet review, its spending teams have had a role in analysing and challenging departments' suggestions for how to improve returns on assets and reduce liabilities. But teams' engagement with the balance sheet review varies and this work has yet to make a difference to the way spending teams monitor departments:

- Some teams brought in senior staff with greater expertise to support the balance sheet review; others delegated it to less experienced staff.
- When identifying potential risks, spending teams focus mainly on in-year and medium-term spending risks – our review of a sample of risk registers showed they rarely flagged balance sheet risks that have no short-term effect on spending.

Supporting longer-term planning

1.18 HM Treasury points to two developments to improve long-term planning. In both cases it is too early to judge their impact:

- In July 2018, the National Infrastructure Commission – established by HM Treasury to make recommendations on long-term infrastructure needs – published its first national infrastructure assessment, including setting out a prioritised framework for long-term investment.
- The National Productivity Investment Fund launched in 2016 and committed funding to 2023-24. It is designed to provide additional investment in housing, infrastructure, and research and development and thereby help boost long-term productivity. At Budget 2018, the government increased its budget from £31 billion to £37 billion.[25]

23 HM Treasury, *Treasury Minutes: Government responses to the Committee of Public Accounts: Sessions 2010-12, 2012-13, 2013-14, 2014-15, 2015-16 and 2016-17 and progress on Government Cash Management*, Cm 9566, January 2018; HC Committee of Public Accounts, *The Government Balance Sheet, Nineteenth Report of Session* 2016-17, HC 485, October 2016; International Monetary Fund, *United Kingdom – Fiscal transparency evaluation*, IMF Country Report No. 16/351, November 2016, available at: www.imf.org/external/pubs/ft/scr/2016/cr16351.pdf; Comptroller and Auditor General, *Evaluating the government balance sheet: borrowing*, Session 2017–2019, HC 526, National Audit Office, November 2017.

24 HM Treasury, *Budget 2018*, HC 1629, 29 October 2018.

25 HM Treasury, *Budget 2018*, HC 1629, 29 October 2018.

1.19 HM Treasury has reformed areas of long-term spending such as pensions and has agreed longer-term planning horizons with a number of departments, underpinned by a guaranteed minimum level of funding:

- The NHS will receive an average 3.4% a year real-terms increase in funding, equivalent to an additional £20.5 billion, over the next five years to support a 10-year plan. The plan and how HM Treasury will monitor its delivery are still being developed.
- The Ministry of Defence's 2015 Spending Review settlement agreed a 0.5% real-terms annual budget increase to support a 10-year forward plan. The Ministry of Defence introduced the Equipment Plan in 2012 following a period of poor financial management, during which a significant gap developed between forecast funding and costs across the defence programme.[26] We have reported for a second year that the Equipment Plan is unaffordable. While awaiting the results of its Modernising Defence Programme, which will include an assessment of future equipment and support needs, the Ministry of Defence has focused on making the first year of the Plan (2018-19) affordable and addressing short-term funding gaps.
- Some £15 billion of financial support over the next five years for housing in the 2017 Autumn Budget. This is split between a number of different programmes. But HM Treasury has not yet agreed with the Ministry of Housing, Communities & Local Government how overall performance will be monitored.
- Five-year funding settlements with both Network Rail and Highways England, with the aim of increasing funding certainty.

1.20 Funding commitments such as these provide stability and a longer horizon within which departments and delivery bodies can set goals for improvement (Figure 1). The next part of this report looks at progress since 2016 with the detailed medium-term business planning that is needed to deliver on such long-term goals.

26 Comptroller and Auditor General, Ministry of Defence, *The Equipment Plan 2018 to 2028*, Session 2017–2019, HC 1621, National Audit Office, November 2018.

Part Two

The evolution of medium-term business planning

2.1 In 2016 we recommended that government retain and further develop the then new approach to business planning which is based around single departmental plans (SDPs).[27] SDPs are intended to help departments make choices about what must be delivered within the spending limits they have been set in the spending review, plan business over the medium-term and manage their performance.

2.2 This part examines progress on:

- establishing SDPs as an enduring part of government's framework;
- embedding the approach to business planning;
- progress with business planning in departments;
- overall maturity of departments' business planning; and
- SDPs and the challenge of the UK's exit from the European Union (EU).

Establishing SDPs as an enduring part of government's framework

2.3 The Cabinet Office's Implementation Unit has continued to develop the SDP process, working with HM Treasury's Planning and Performance Team and the functions. The 2017 general election, ministerial changes in the Cabinet Office and key delivery departments, and the additional priorities associated with the UK's exit from the EU could have led to SDPs being dropped. But in 2017 the Cabinet Office and HM Treasury confirmed to Parliament they would maintain SDPs as an enduring basis for government's planning and performance framework.[28]

27 Comptroller and Auditor General, *Government's management of its performance: progress with single departmental plans*, Session 2016-17, HC 872, National Audit Office, July 2016.

28 Cabinet Office and HM Treasury, letter to the chair, HC Committee of Public Accounts, 28 November 2017; Cabinet Office and HM Treasury, *The government's planning and performance framework*, December 2017, available at: www.gov.uk/government/publications/planning-and-performance-framework/the-governments-planning-and-performance-framework.

2.4 Nearly all departments produced draft SDPs for 2018-19 and shared them with the Cabinet Office and HM Treasury by May 2018. All departments also produced a public plan in May 2018.[29] By September 2018:

- 13 SDPs were agreed by the centre of government without conditions;
- two were agreed on condition that the department provided more detail;
- two were not agreed. The centre of government set out what the departments needed to do before submitting a revised plan; and
- formal commitment letters between ministers in spending departments and ministers at the centre of government had yet to go out, although the 2018-19 financial year was already half-way through.[30]

Embedding the approach to business planning

2.5 The Implementation Unit is working with a range of stakeholders to embed sustainable change in government's business planning capability (**Figure 7**). It wants to help departments to improve themselves, rather than to impose change from the centre of government, which suggests it has learned from past experience.[31] Some departments have now realigned the structure and timing of their internal business planning and reporting arrangements with the SDP regime. Respondents to our 2018 survey of finance and planning officials, across 18 departments, indicated that SDPs are becoming integral to the way departments manage themselves, though there is room for further improvement (**Figure 8** on page 34).

Progress with business planning in departments

2.6 In 2016 we saw signs that departments were making progress in improving their business planning, although from a low base.[32] Our survey results suggest all aspects of business planning have improved since then (**Figure 9** on page 35). However, the responses indicate plenty of scope for progress, and continuing areas of weakness, particularly in understanding the relationship between inputs, outputs and outcomes, and the use of performance data for decision-making. Our discussions with case study departments and the Cabinet Office's quality assurance of all departments' SDPs both broadly confirm these areas of strength and weakness (**Figure 10** on page 36).

29 Cabinet Office, *Building a country that works for everyone: the government's plan*, December 2017, available at: www.gov.uk/government/collections/a-country-that-works-for-everyone-the-governments-plan

30 These letters were issued in October 2018.

31 "Previous reforms have tended to fall short of real transformation because of a lack of sustained political leadership, a lack of engagement of civil servants within departments in driving change themselves, and a lack of clarity and rigour in targeting and tracking the benefits." Comptroller and Auditor General, *Memorandum on the 2012 Civil Service Reform Plan*, Session 2012-13, HC 915, National Audit Office, January 2013.

32 Comptroller and Auditor General, *Government's management of its performance: progress with single departmental plans*, Session 2016-17, HC 872, National Audit Office, July 2016.

Figure 7

The corporate centre of government is working in a coordinated way to improve business planning

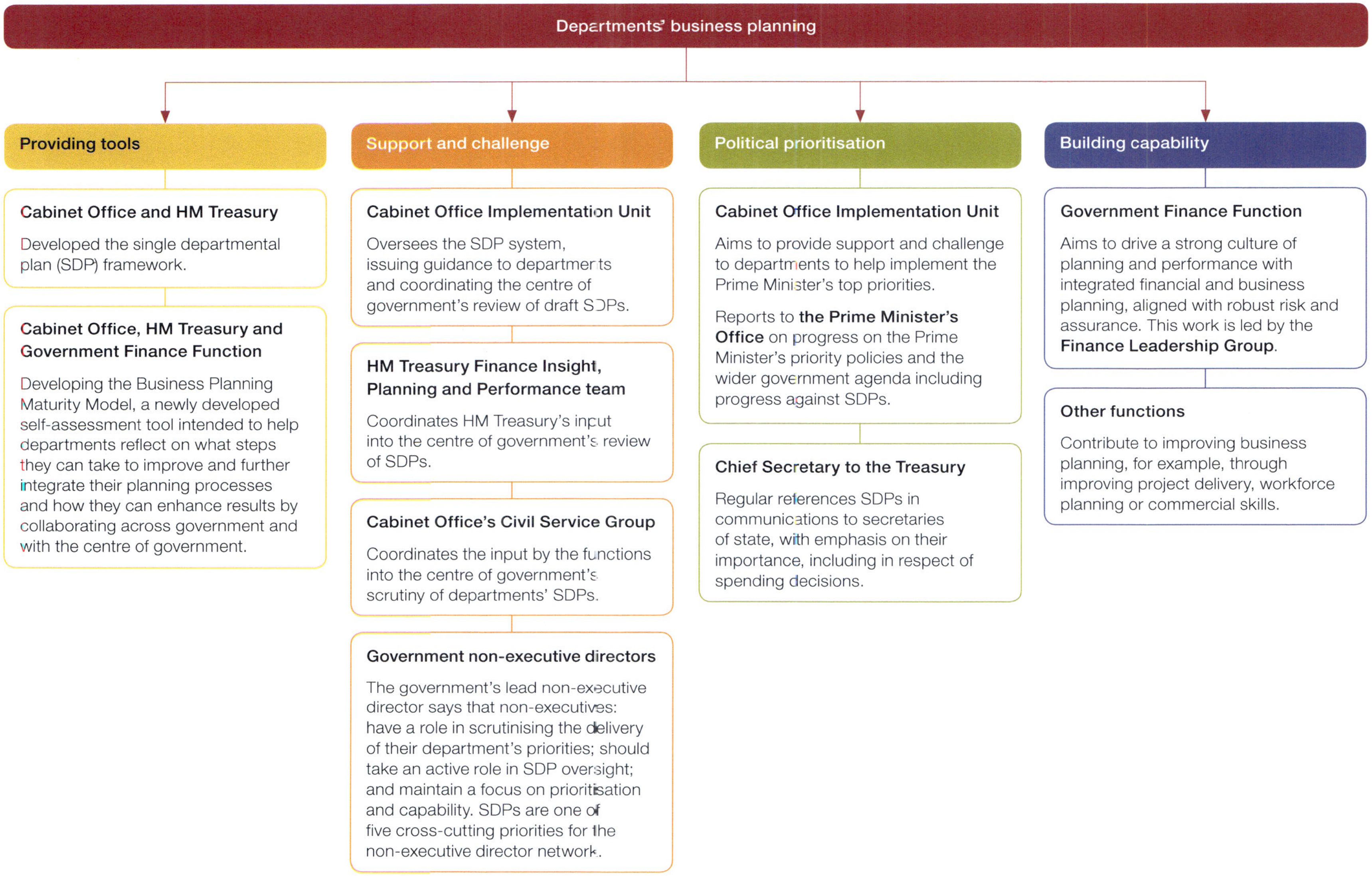

Source: National Audit Office

Figure 8
Status and use of single departmental plans in departments

To what extent do you agree that the production of the department's single departmental plan was an integral part of your department's business planning activities? (n=59)

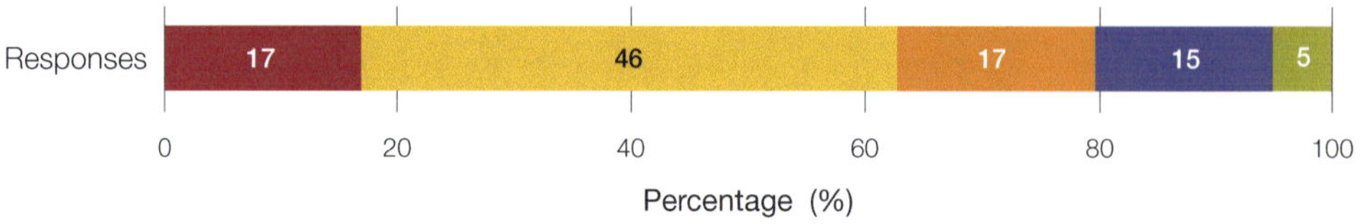

- Strongly agree
- Agree
- Neither agree nor disagree
- Disagree
- Strongly disagree

In your experience, is the unpublished internal single departmental plan used by senior management for decision-making? (n=62)

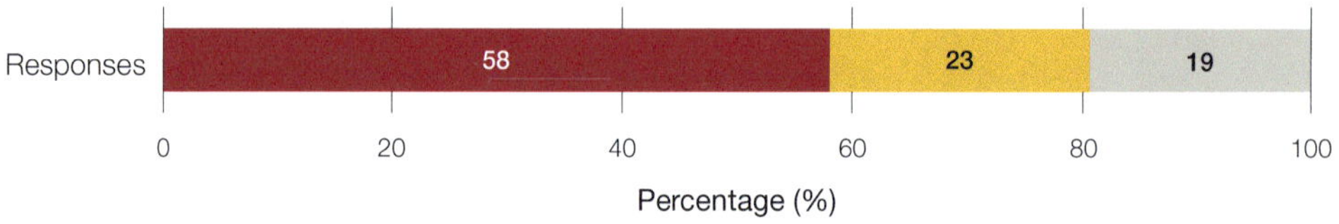

- Yes, it is used for management purposes
- No, we use a separate plan
- Don't know

Note

1 Percentages may not add up to exactly 100 due to rounding.

Source: National Audit Office survey of staff involved in business planning across departments

Figure 9
Those involved in business planning report that planning was better in 2018-19 than in previous years

Please rate the strength of your department in the following aspects of business planning

Notes

1 'Strong' is the sum of respondents who either chose very strong or strong. 'Weak' is the sum of respondents who either chose very weak or weak.

2 Percentages may not add up to exactly 100 due to rounding.

Source: National Audit Office survey of 57 to 62 staff involved in business planning across departments

Figure 10

The Cabinet Office's centre review panels' quality assessments of 17 draft single departmental plans

The Cabinet Office's quality assurance of departments' single departmental plans identified areas of strength and weakness

Criterion applied	Number of departments against each quality rating					Comments
Clear objectives and sub-objectives	9	5	1	2	0	Nearly all departments set out clear objectives and sub-objectives.
Specific milestones or deliverables	4	7	3	3	0	The panel prompted several departments to provide more milestones. Some milestones did not have dates attached.
Measurable performance indicators	7	1	6	3	0	The panel advised a number of departments to develop their performance indicators, and commended one. In some, the link between milestones and indicators was not clear enough.
Includes public commitments	13	3	1	0	0	Several departments had to be reminded to include all manifesto commitments.
Medium-term financial and workforce plans	7	5	5	0	0	Some departments did not include a medium-term financial and workforce plan. Others did, but it did not cover the whole plan period.
Functional plans	10	3	2	2	0	Most draft plans were clear about the department's contribution to the cross-government agenda to improve common functions, for example estates, digital, HR, commercial.

Source: National Audit Office analysis of Cabinet Office data

2.7 Departments are at different levels of maturity in business planning and facing different pressures, which has led them to prioritise different improvements (**Figure 11**, **Figure 12** and **Figure 13** on page 38). Our discussions and document review at seven departments indicate that the SDP approach is helping departments to conduct business planning in a more professional, informed, integrated way, involving internal stakeholders more fully. Departments told us it has helped them to set out defined, unambiguous objectives, and clarify internal accountabilities for delivery.

2.8 The Cabinet Office gave departments two rounds of feedback on their single departmental plans. The feedback contained suggestions from across the Cabinet Office and HM Treasury, including the functions, such as the Infrastructure and Projects Authority, and spending teams. Among departmental staff responding to our survey, more than half considered the centre of government had added value to their department's business planning (**Figure 14** on page 39).

Figure 11

Improving measures of performance in the Ministry of Justice

The Ministry's Single Departmental Plan (SDP) includes milestones and metrics against which system progress can be measured

The Ministry of Justice works with a number of government and non-government bodies across the justice system. We previously reported that because there was no common view of what success looks like in the criminal justice system, organisations may not act in the best interests of the whole system.

The Ministry's SDP sets out the links between strategic objectives, policy initiatives, front-line activities and resources. For each strategic objective, there are one or more priority areas, which are further broken down into sub-objectives with an associated aim/outcome and a plan for delivery. The SDP includes a framework of milestones and metrics, linked to sub-objectives, which are monitored throughout the year to track progress and provide accountability. Each metric has an expected target level and the milestones provide a timetable for delivery.

The Ministry told us the development of the SDP and performance framework has helped it make better decisions about planning and spending and enhanced its management of its own performance. It is shared with staff to help them see how their work contributes to objectives.

Extracts from the Ministry's internal and external SDPs, showing structure of plan

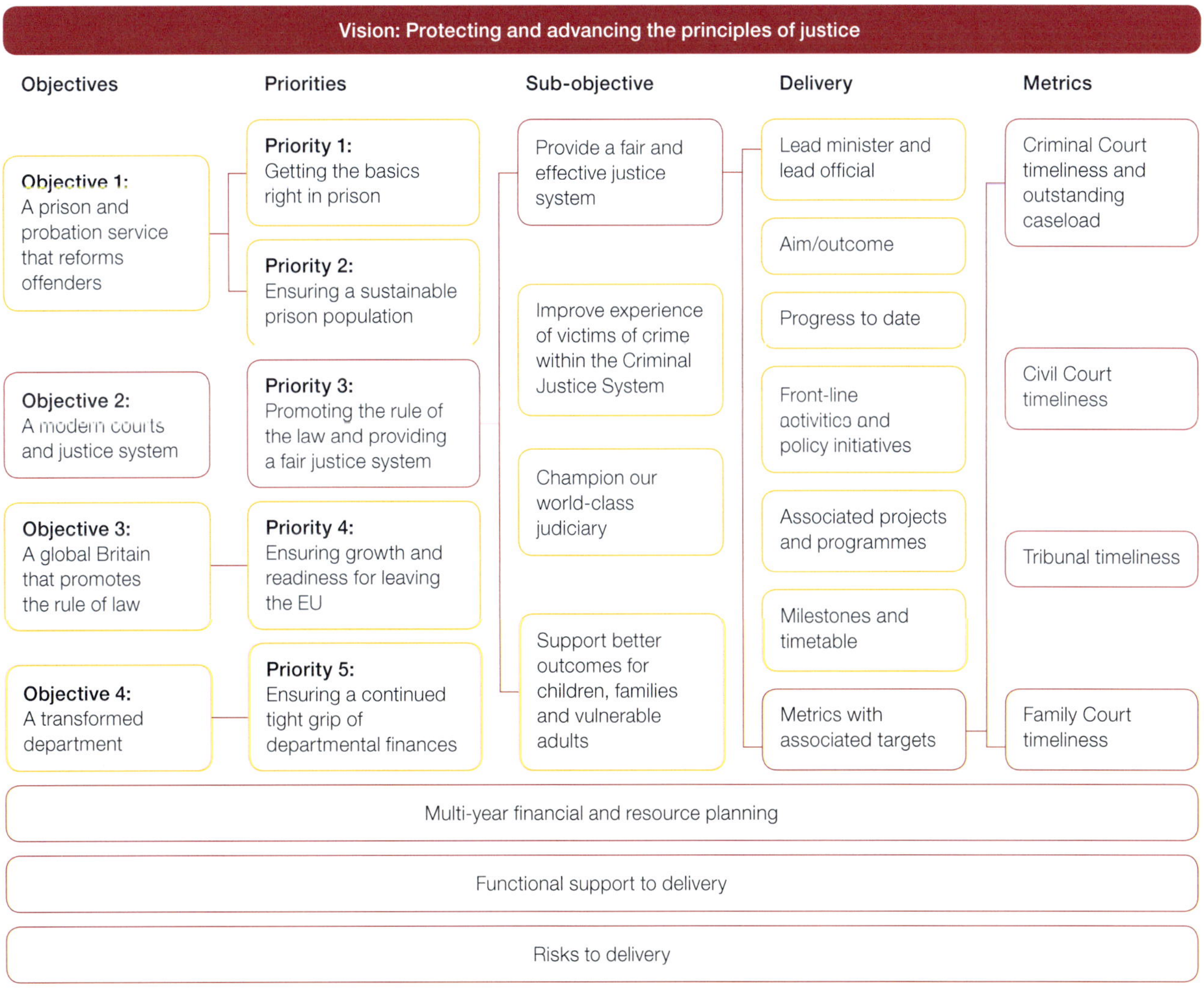

Note

1 Comptroller and Auditor General, *Efficiency in the criminal justice system*, Session 2015-16, HC 852, National Audit Office, March 2016.

Source: National Audit Office, Ministry of Justice

Figure 12

Using internal challenge to improve business planning rigour at the Department for Work & Pensions

The Department has built in expert challenge to the business planning process

The Department for Work & Pensions (DWP) has redesigned its business planning process to introduce greater rigour and accurate forecasting of spending, and challenge optimism bias in planning. The main driver of these changes was the need to improve in-year budget management; DWP has also aligned the new approach with the production of the Single Departmental Plan (SDP) in late spring each year.

In DWP's 'summer planning' exercise, each directorate addresses strategic priorities for the following 3-4 years, which is the subject of internal challenge:

- Finance business partners attached to each directorate provide ongoing challenge, for example on cost estimates.
- DWP's central finance team reviews each plan and requests further development where necessary.
- A formal challenge meeting is chaired by the finance director general. It may recommend further detail, for example a better understanding of cost drivers, or testing of assumptions or alternative scenarios.
- If elements of the plan need further development, the central finance function will retain funding for this element. This earmarks the funding but it will not be released until the directorate has completed the extra work.

The 'winter planning' exercise focuses solely on the following financial year. Plans are updated across the organisation with the aim of allowing DWP to set a balanced budget for the following year.

Source: National Audit Office and Department for Work & Pensions

Figure 13

Engaging staff with departmental objectives in the Department for Digital, Culture, Media & Sport

The Department used its Single Departmental Plan (SDP) to set out strategic objectives to large numbers of new staff

The Department has deliberately promoted its 2018-19 SDP as a way of refreshing staff's understanding of the strategic objectives to which they contribute, and integrating newly arrived staff into the organisational culture. Following the move of government's digital policy responsibility to the Department from the Cabinet Office in July 2017, it has grown in staff numbers from 656 in 2016-17 to 887 in 2017-18. The Department told us that 14 of its 17 directors were new in post over the course of 18 months.

The corporate strategy team produced a video, ran workshops and provided guidance to line managers, to help staff set team and personal objectives that would support the strategic objectives in the SDP. The Department intends to measure success through its staff engagement survey in 2019.

Source: National Audit Office and Department for Digital, Culture, Media & Sport

Figure 14

Challenge and added value by the central government on single departmental plans (SDPs)

Departments most often mentioned that they valued the Cabinet Office's:

- constructive challenge;
- consistent framework and guidance; and
- cross-government peer support network.

We saw examples of Cabinet Office:

- prompting links between departments' plans. For example, making sure the Department of Health & Social Care's SDP made the link between the work it does on life sciences, and the Department for Business, Energy & Industrial Strategy's work in the same area;
- pushing for longer-term financial and delivery planning – some departments had only included one year of financial plans;
- requiring manifesto commitments to be included, where these were missing; and
- requiring clarity on departments' contributions to whole-of-government commitments, such as supporting small businesses or digital policy.

Survey respondents were keen to see the centre of government do more, including:

- take a longer-term approach to funding to support better planning;
- show deeper understanding of individual departments and their challenges;
- provide more evidence-based, realistic challenge;
- share clearer and earlier guidance; and
- build stronger planning capability within the centre of government and departments.

Source: National Audit Office analysis of Cabinet Office documents; interviews with its Implementation Unit staff; and analysis of most common responses to our survey of staff involved in business planning, on the question "thinking now about the future, what more would you like to see the centre of government do to support your department in long-term business planning?"

Overall maturity of departments' business planning

2.9 In 2018, Sir Ian Cheshire, Government Lead Non-Executive Director, said:

> "Good planning is essential to delivery… especially in setting real priorities. I encourage all non-executives to play their part in the development of SDPs reflecting the strategic agenda, with realistic implementation plans and clear resources set against desired results."[33]

The evolution of SDPs, and in particular the introduction of mandatory medium-term financial plans in 2017-18, represents a promising start towards the ideal of realistic planning, with clear resources and real priorities, as set out by the government's lead non-executive director, but they come from a low starting point.

33 HM Government, *Government planning and performance. Guidance for departments on Single Departmental Plans*, October 2017.

2.10 Not all business plans were comprehensive. In some cases departments' draft SDPs did not cover all their activities or did not include all the information required in the central guidance. The Implementation Unit noted that, for example, the Ministry of Housing, Communities & Local Government's SDP did not include commitments in the *Housing white paper*; and the Ministry of Defence's draft SDP did not provide sufficient detail on the £7.4 billion efficiency programme.

2.11 Not all business plans integrated activity planning with resource planning. We recommended in 2017 that the Cabinet Office should ensure departmental workforce plans, functional plans and SDPs are integrated.[34] Not all departments were able to produce the required medium-term financial and workforce plans in 2018, and others were not complete, or did not match the timeframe of the whole plan, suggesting that departments are not yet planning in a way that matches what they propose to deliver with the resources available to deliver it. Only 43% of respondents agreed that their 2018-19 SDP was clear on how the delivery of objectives would be supported by financial and workforce resources.

> "Our department, and I suspect other departments too, are good at producing plans, but less adept at planning – particularly when it comes to making difficult choices about what things to do and how to do them. There is a need to build capability in strategic and business planning and to integrate financial and workforce planning more closely with them."
>
> Survey respondent.

2.12 Not all business plans were affordable. A number of departments told us their overriding objective in their business planning was to stay within their current year's budget, having relied for several years on mid-year injections of funding from HM Treasury. This focus on annual affordability is important but underlines how far some departments are from being able to make longer-term plans, and runs the risk of simply pushing unaffordable commitments into the future.

> "...[the] focus on annual planning detracts from 3–5 year planning, which is urgently needed to upgrade and upskill the Department's people."
>
> Non-executive director, survey respondent.

> "Current system (which penalises even the smallest overspend against control targets) leads to excessive conservatism and poor forecasting."
>
> Non-executive director, survey respondent.

34 Comptroller and Auditor General, *Capability in the civil service*, Session 2016-17, HC 919, National Audit Office, March 2017.

2.13 The Cabinet Office and HM Treasury, with support from the Infrastructure and Projects Authority, have begun to test departments' costings, and examine overall affordability of their plans; we understand that non-executive directors and the chief executive of the civil service have also provided challenge at board level. However, efforts to assess overall affordability, deliverability and risk across government's plans in aggregate could go further. The Cabinet Office has worked to improve alignment between the strategic plans of the civil service functions and departments' SDPs, which should produce a cross-government picture of specialist capability, although not all the functions have yet produced fully developed plans.

2.14 Not all business plans reflected real prioritisation. Staff involved in business planning continue to say that any efforts to reprioritise depend on ministerial support if they are to be effective.[35]

> "...stopping deliverables with major political backing remains difficult, even in the face of Brexit pressures."
>
> Survey respondent.

> "...the tendency is to try to do everything, spreading teams more thinly rather than stopping or delaying de-prioritised activities."
>
> Survey respondent.

While survey respondents felt that criteria used by their departments for making decisions about priorities had improved (Figure 9), only 53% said their department accurately aligned planned deliverables with capacity and capability (**Figure 15** overleaf). Only 45% of staff were confident that their department actually stopped or substantially delayed deliverables, where a prioritisation exercise supported it (**Figure 16** overleaf). We found few examples of the centre of government questioning the high number of priorities listed in SDPs.

SDPs and the challenge of the UK's exit from the EU

2.15 The Committee of Public Accounts was particularly concerned that departments have still not faced up to the need to re-prioritise existing activity to make space for work related to EU Exit, and saw this as a key test of the SDP approach. The Committee called on departments to set out evidence of what they had de-prioritised in their spring 2018 SDPs, but government did not agree and did not provide a list of activities dropped.[36] The Cabinet Office told us that work in this area is progressing – for example it has since set up a new team to provide central support to specific priority projects and programmes with the highest EU Exit delivery risks across departments.

35 Analysis of the most recurring themes from 40 comments to our survey question: "In your opinion, does your department actually stop or substantially delay deliverables, where a prioritisation exercise supports it?"

36 Committee of Public Accounts, *Exiting the European Union*. Eighteenth Report of Session 2017–19, HC 467, February 2018; HM Treasury, *Treasury Minutes: Government response to the Committee of Public Accounts on the Twelfth to the Nineteenth reports from Session 2017–2019*, Cm 9596, March 2018.

Figure 15
Aligning priorities with departments' capacity and capability

To what extent do you agree that prioritisation in your department has accurately aligned planned deliverables with capacity and capability? (n=64)

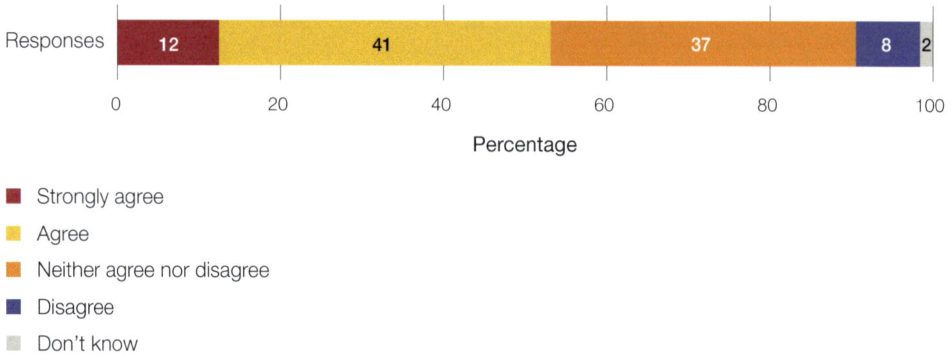

Notes

1 By 'capacity' we mean having enough people and resources. By 'capability' we mean having the ability to implement policy effectively, for which the civil service needs people with the right skills.

2 Percentages may not add up to exactly 100 due to rounding.

Source: National Audit Office survey of staff involved in business planning across departments

Figure 16
Prevalence of re- and de-prioritisation

In your opinion, does your department actually stop or substantially delay deliverables, where a prioritisation exercise supports it? (n=64)

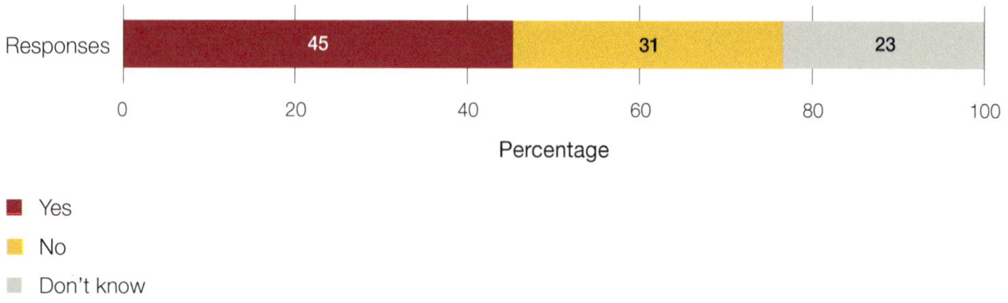

Note

1 Percentages may not add up to exactly 100 due to rounding.

Source: National Audit Office survey of staff involved in business planning across departments

2.16 There were 20 applications to HM Treasury for additional funding for EU Exit activities in 2018-19. Our review of the applications showed that few departments had reprioritised funding internally to support EU Exit work.[37] Some said they had already used up all the scope for cuts to meet their 2015 Spending Review settlements.

2.17 In our previous work on implementing EU Exit, we saw examples of departments making tactical adjustments to meet immediate pressures, but there was little sign of strategic reprioritisation across the whole of a department's programme of work.[38,39] Of the 319 EU Exit work streams across government,[40] many will stretch over a number of years or permanently increase a department's workload, but only one-third of survey respondents thought EU Exit may lead to a permanent change in the way departments plan their business.

2.18 DExEU worked with all departments affected by EU Exit, to help them decide on priorities within their EU Exit portfolio. It ran two 'stocktake' exercises with these departments in 2017 to examine their readiness for exiting the EU, agree prioritisation issues, and identify any barriers to progress and actions to address them.[41] We have seen examples of departments, such as the Department for Transport and the Department for Environment, Food & Rural Affairs forced to prioritise within their EU Exit work, because of finite resources or time.[42,43] However, it was up to departments to determine how to fit the additional deliveries in with their existing workload.

2.19 The only department to explicitly inform the Committee of Public Accounts that it is dropping existing work is HM Revenue & Customs (HMRC).[44] This was mainly to deal with the impact of the UK's exit from the EU on HMRC but also to ensure its transformation plans could be delivered. HMRC's prioritisation exercise allowed it to release 51 staff for work to prepare for the UK's exit from the EU. HMRC has devised an approach to assessing all new commitments against its strategic objectives, to help it prioritise its work portfolio (**Figure 17** overleaf).

37 In November 2017 HM Treasury invited departments to bid for EU Exit funding and asked them to show how they were reprioritising existing resources before calling for more. The Chief Secretary to the Treasury, Written Statement HCWS540, 13 March 2018, available at: www.parliament.uk/business/publications/written-questions-answers-statements/written-statement/Commons/2018-03-13/HCWS540/

38 Comptroller and Auditor General, *Progress in implementing the UK's Exit from the European Union*, Session 2017–2019, HC 1498, National Audit Office, September 2018.

39 Comptroller and Auditor General, *Implementing the UK's Exit from the European Union: The Department for International Trade*, Session 2017–2019, HC 713, National Audit Office, January 2018.

40 Comptroller and Auditor General, *Progress in Implementing EU Exit*, Session 2017–2019, HC 1498, National Audit Office, September 2018.

41 Comptroller and Auditor General, *Implementing the UK's exit from the European Union: The Department for Exiting the European Union and the centre of government*, Session 2017–2019, HC 593, National Audit Office, November 2017; Comptroller and Auditor General, *Implementing the UK's exit from the European Union: The Foreign and Commonwealth Office*, Session 2017–2019, HC 899, National Audit Office, April 2018; Comptroller and Auditor General, *Implementing the UK's Exit from the European Union: The Department for International Trade*, Session 2017–2019, HC 713, National Audit Office, January 2018.

42 Comptroller and Auditor General, *Implementing the UK's Exit from the European Union*, Session 2017–2019, HC 1125, National Audit Office, July 2018.

43 Comptroller and Auditor General, *Progress in implementing the UK's Exit from the European Union*, Session 2017–2019, HC 1498, National Audit Office, September 2018.

44 Comptroller and Auditor General, 'Report by the Comptroller and Auditor General', in *HM Revenue & Customs: Annual Report and Accounts 2017-18*, Session 2017–2019, HC 1222, July 2018.

Figure 17

HM Revenue & Customs' prioritisation exercise

The Department devised an approach to help it make decisions about which activities to prioritise

HM Revenue & Customs (HMRC) is further developing its understanding of how the projects in its transformation portfolio relate to its overall vision for transforming its business. It is using a 'portfolio alignment tool' to enable it to map its high-level strategic objectives to its transformation plans and the work it has committed to carrying out. HMRC considers that this analysis will help it to identify potential gaps in delivery of required capabilities to achieve its vision. It will enable it to provide impact assessments to support decisions on which activities to prioritise and what work to introduce into its portfolio. This could provide learning for the rest of government.

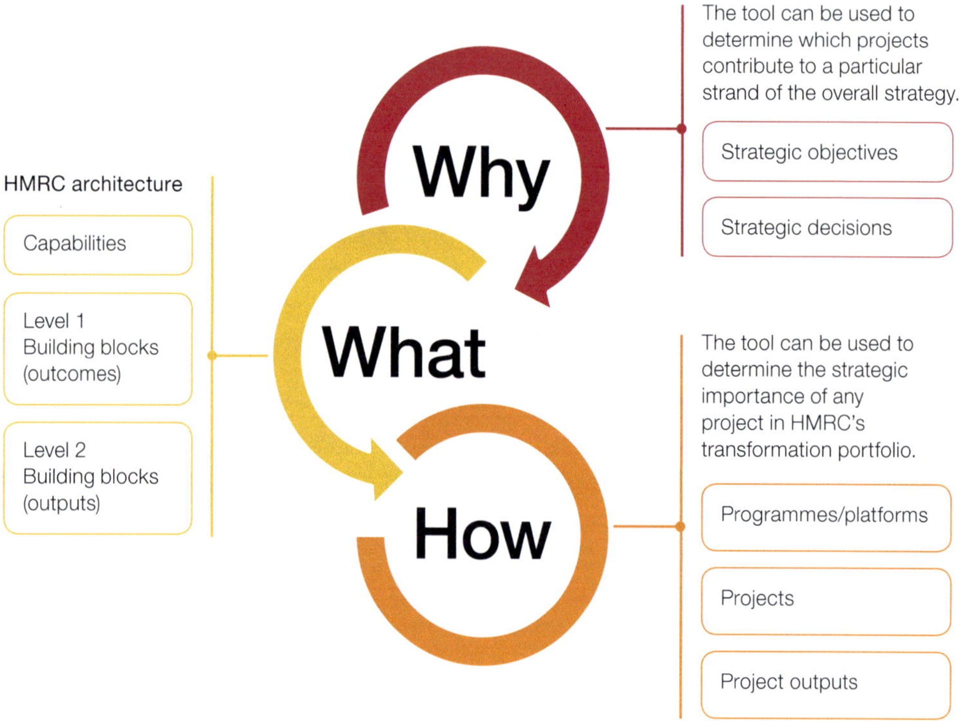

Source: Comptroller and Auditor General, *HM Revenue & Customs Annual Report and Accounts 2017-18*, Session 2017-19, HC 1222, National Audit Office, July 2018

Part Three

The evolution of HM Treasury's approach to managing spending in the short-term

3.1 HM Treasury's scrutiny of departmental spending is an essential part of managing public money effectively. HM Treasury oversight and control is needed to balance fiscal and other objectives and ensure basic financial management discipline. As priorities change and circumstances shift, so government needs to be able to adjust its spending plans and resources, whether through periodic spending reviews, annual budgets or in-year adjustments. It needs a clear view of the impact that such short-term changes have on medium- and long-term value for money.

3.2 Our 2016 report highlighted the transactional nature of the relationship between departments and HM Treasury spending teams during the 2015 Spending Review. We recommended that HM Treasury should engage more openly with departments, to allow better discussions about departments' ability to deliver; make more use of expertise across the centre of government, challenge and understand departments' plans; and improve its insights into departments' spending in between spending reviews.[45]

3.3 In its response, HM Treasury agreed that it would need to look again at the way it works and spend more time focusing on information on performance.[46] This part covers spending teams':

- role in managing spending;
- relationship with departments;
- capability, capacity and use of others' expertise; and
- monitoring of departments.

45 Comptroller and Auditor General, *Spending Review 2015*, Session 2016-17, HC 571, National Audit Office, July 2016.
46 Comptroller and Auditor General, *Government's management of its performance: progress with single departmental plans*, Session 2016-17, HC 872, National Audit Office, July 2016, paragraph 2.19.

Spending teams' role in managing spending

3.4 The job of controlling spending is a major part of spending teams' relationships with departments. The work of spending teams informs HM Treasury's General Expenditure Policy team in its analysis of the overall spending position. This team is responsible for controlling public spending, and making sure that departments stay within the spending limits and rules that the government sets. HM Treasury organises its 20 spending teams into six groups whose overall structure is broadly unchanged since 2016. Together, they make up around one-fifth of HM Treasury's total workforce. Spending teams' remit is broad (Figure 2). Their core guidance and processes centre around spending control and scrutinising and approving project and programme spending outside of departments' delegated limits, with the aim of delivering value for money.[47]

3.5 The International Monetary Fund's analysis shows the UK has been the most successful country in the European Union (EU) at meeting its spending forecasts in the past 15 years (**Figure 18**). The Office for Budget Responsibility's latest forecasts indicate that HM Treasury is on track to meet its key fiscal targets to reduce both the deficit – the gap between what government receives and spends – and public sector net debt.[48]

3.6 There will sometimes be a need to adjust plans and funding as circumstances, assumptions about demand for services, or policy priorities change. But, other than significant unforeseen needs, HM Treasury expects departments to manage within their budgets. Therefore, if business planning proves to be over-optimistic, this can drive short-term cost-cutting at all levels of government, and jeopardise value for money in the longer term, as we and the Committee have found (**Figure 19** on page 48). The Institute for Fiscal Studies has cautioned that controlling spending in the short-term does not equal long-term control, and government risks big pressures building up as some public services start to struggle.[49]

Spending teams' relationship with departments

3.7 Overall, departments are positive about their relationship with spending teams – 92% of survey respondents agreed that spending team staff actively seek to build a constructive and transparent relationship (**Figure 20** on page 49). In addition, 83% of survey respondents said that spending teams understood departments' issues, risks and challenges. Departments we interviewed described relationships as reasonable or good. Good relationships were linked to open and collaborative engagement, and more data-sharing and contact with the spending team. Departments were, however, less positive about flexibility of financial control and appropriateness of delegated spending limits. One department said that the spending team should "lift some ring-fences", and that the spending team should "reduce the number of occasions when we need their approval, or turn around those approvals much more quickly".

47 HM Treasury, *Managing Public Money*, July 2013 with annexes revised as at March 2018; HM Treasury, *The Green Book – Central government guidance on appraisal and evaluation*, 2018; and, HM Treasury, *Treasury approvals process for programmes and projects*, November 2016

48 Office for Budget Responsibility, *Economic and Fiscal Outlook*, October 2018.

49 Institute for Fiscal Studies, *The planning and control of UK public expenditure 1993–2015*, July 2018, available at: www.ifs.org.uk/publications/13155

Figure 18

Average expenditure forecast error, 2000–2015

The International Monetary Fund's analysis shows that the UK has been the most successful country in the European Union at meeting its spending forecasts in the last 15 years

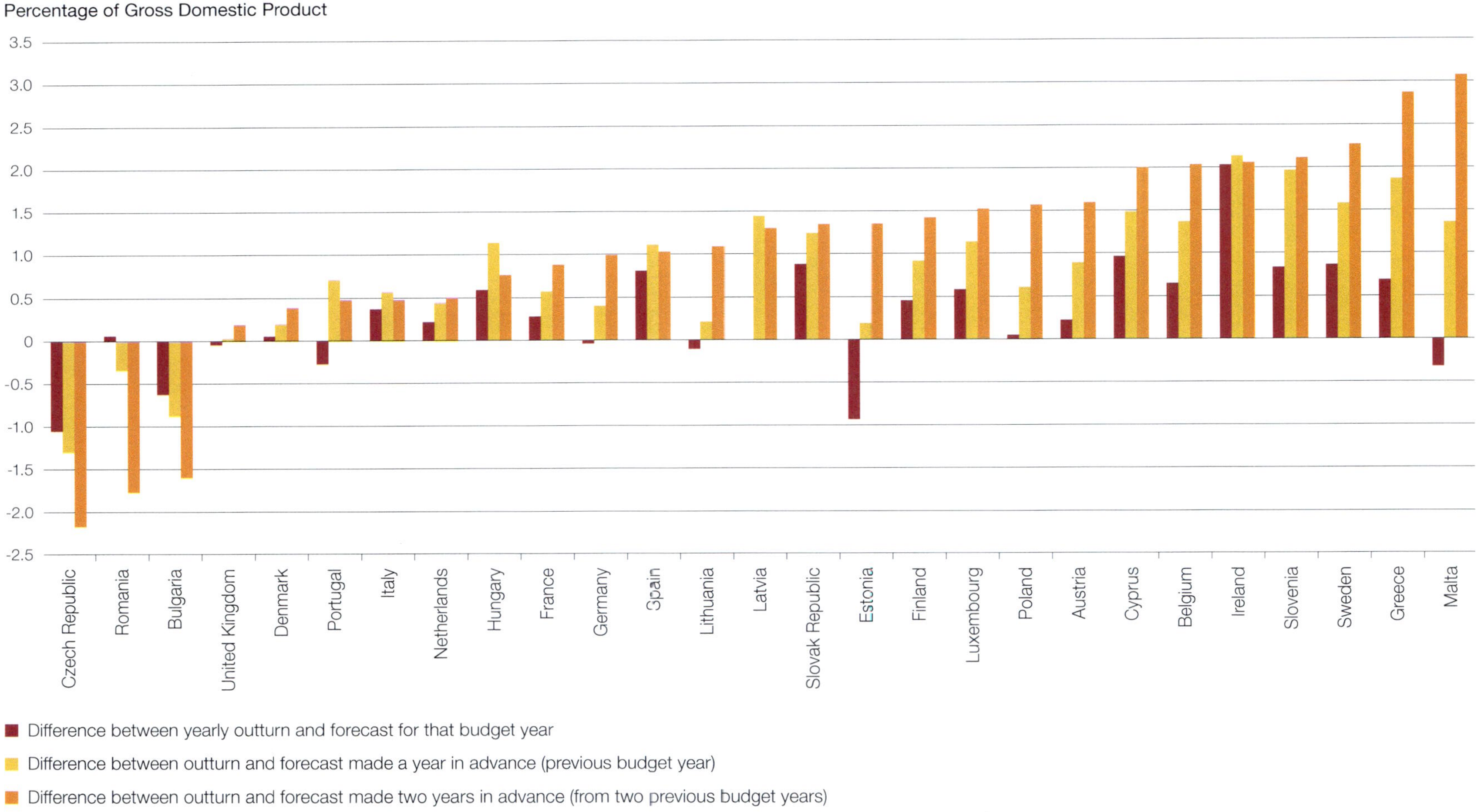

Source: International Monetary Fund, *United Kingdom – Fiscal transparency evaluation*, IMF Country Report No. 16/351, November 2016

Figure 19

Short-term decisions that affect long-term value for money: examples

Area of service	Committee of Public Accounts or National Audit Office conclusion
The adult social care workforce in England, February 2018[1]	The Department is not doing enough to support the development of a sustainable care workforce. Both providers and commissioners from local authorities told us that **current funding constraints mean they must prioritise the provision of care in the short term over offering extensive long-term support for learning and career development to their staff.**
Financial sustainability in the further education sector, December 2015[2]	The departments and funding agencies[3] sometimes make decisions without properly understanding the impact on learners, nor the impact on colleges' ability to compete with other education providers. Colleges face a number of substantial external challenges, some of which are exacerbated by the actions of the departments and their funding agencies. These include **very late funding decisions, including a funding cut only days before the start of the 2015/16 academic year.**
Defence Equipment Plan, January 2018[4]	To manage the short-term unaffordability of its Equipment Plan, the Ministry of Defence has delayed certain equipment and support programmes and reduced how much it spends on support. **Delays to some programmes have led to existing equipment being used for longer, which creates greater uncertainty and potentially cost.** Given savings measures, and as equipment is being used for longer, the Royal Navy is increasingly having to take spare parts from other vessels to keep ships and submarines afloat and maintain capability.
Capital spending for schools, April 2017[5]	There is **insufficient focus on routine maintenance to keep school buildings in good condition and prevent more costly problems in the future**. The Department for Education uses its capital funding to address urgent needs, rather than to undertake preventative work, and prioritises repairing, refurbishing or rebuilding schools in the worst condition. Meanwhile, schools have to meet the cost of preventative maintenance and repairing smaller defects from their revenue budgets.
Sustainability and financial performance of acute hospital trusts, March 2016[6]	The 4% efficiency target for trusts set by Monitor and NHS England was driven by the shortage of resources available across the NHS overall. NHS England agreed that **aggressive efficiency targets had caused long-term damage to trusts' financial positions**. It said the new efficiency savings target of 2% from 2016-17 was a "more reasonable" requirement for trusts to deliver.
Sustainability and transformation in the NHS, April 2018[7]	The Department of Health & Social Care used the £1.8 billion Sustainability and Transformation Fund in 2016-17 to address the financial deficit in the trust sector, rather than improving and developing services for patients... HM Treasury gave the Department £337 million additional funding in 2017-18, partly to cope with winter pressures, but this was announced in November 2017, too late for trusts to effectively plan how this would be spent... **These cash injections paper over the cracks in NHS finances rather than achieve lasting improvement.**

Notes

1 Comptroller and Auditor General, *The adult social care workforce in England*, Session 2017–2019, HC 714, National Audit Office, February 2018.

2 HC Committee of Public Accounts, *Overseeing financial sustainability in the further education sector*, Thirteenth Report of Session 2015-16, HC 414, December 2015.

3 The Department for Education, the Department for Business, Energy and Industrial Strategy, the Skills Funding Agency and the Education Funding Agency.

4 Comptroller and Auditor General, *The Equipment Plan 2017 to 2027*, Session 2017–2019, HC 717, National Audit Office, January 2018.

5 HC Committee of Public Accounts, *Capital spending for schools*, Fifty-seventh Report of Session 2016-17, HC 961, April 2017.

6 HC Committee of Public Accounts, *Sustainability and financial performance of acute hospital trusts*, Thirteenth Report of Session 2015-16, HC 709, March 2016.

7 HC Committee of Public Accounts, *Sustainability and transformation in the NHS*, Twenty-ninth Report of Session 2017–2019, HC 793, April 2018.

Source: National Audit Office

Figure 20
Departments' relationship with spending teams

Thinking about your contact with the spending team, to what extent do you agree with the following?
The spending team:

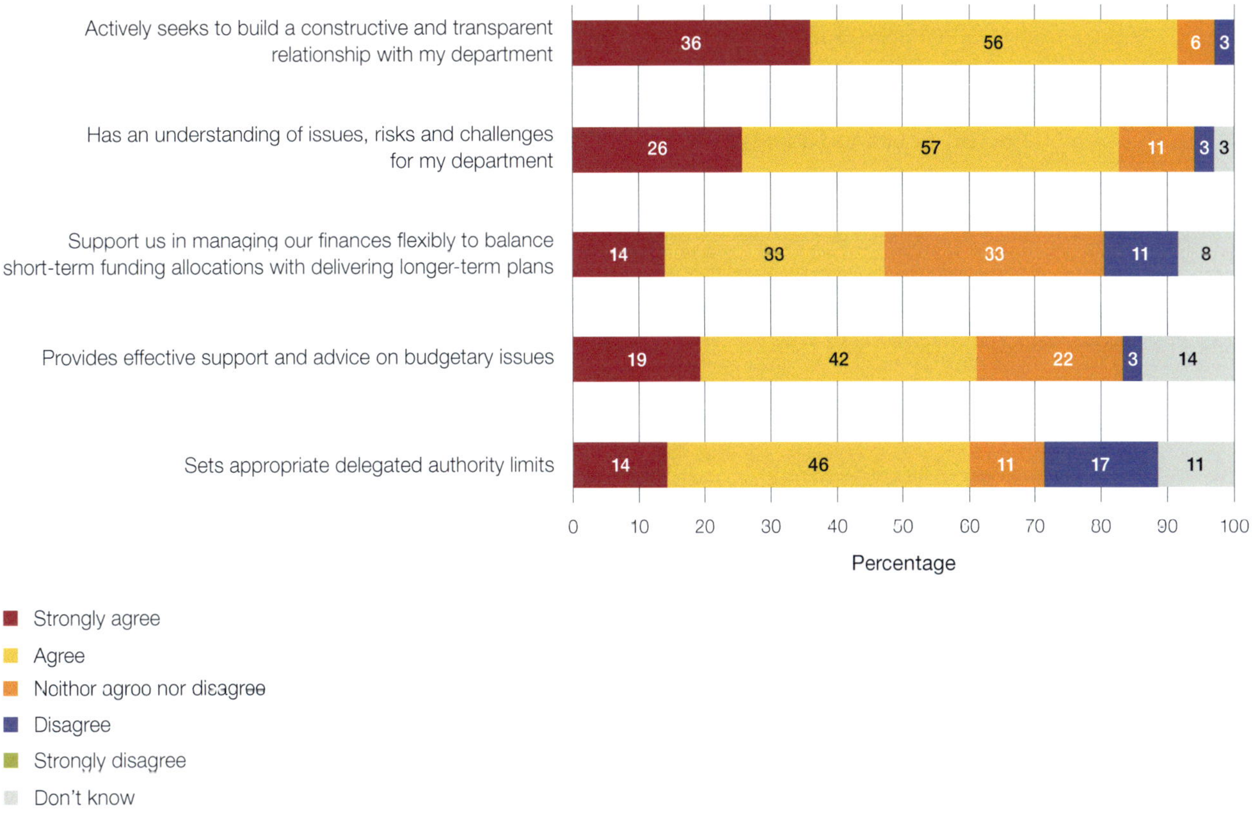

Note

1 Percentages may not add up to exactly 100 due to rounding.

Source: National Audit Office survey of 35 to 36 staff across departments who have direct contact with their department's spending team

3.8 HM Treasury encourages good financial management through adjusting departments' delegated authority limits.[50,51] Departments that demonstrate excellent financial management can be given greater freedom to manage their own resources. This potentially includes the flexibility to move spending between years. HM Treasury has an established process for updating these delegated limits. After Spending Review 2015, in spring 2016, HM Treasury set new limits for seven departments. We noted there have been no changes since then, although the Ministry of Defence – which has the largest delegated limit – reflected that the frequency of its contact with HM Treasury and the focus on committed and uncommitted funding had increased demonstrably as a result of the challenges the Ministry of Defence faces in balancing its budget.

50 Delegated authority limits are where HM Treasury delegates spending authority to departments, subject to upper limits based on the amount of spend on a particular project or programme, and the level of risk involved.

51 HM Treasury, *Improving Spending Control*, April 2012 and HM Treasury, *Review of financial management in government*, December 2013.

Spending teams' capability, capacity and their use of others' expertise

3.9 HM Treasury does not have an overview of the existing skills and experience across its spending teams but highlights influencing skills as crucial, alongside competencies such as delivering value for money, communication and collaboration. Departments were broadly positive about spending teams' skills and capability. Respondents rated spending teams most highly on policy and analytical skills, and least on operational delivery experience (**Figure 21**). Similarly, our interviews in departments reflected on the smart and talented people working in spending teams but highlighted a lack of operational experience, particularly at more junior levels, resulting in a perceived lack of pragmatism when dealing with departments.

Figure 21
Skills and experience of spending teams in effectively monitoring and scrutinising departments

How would you rate the following skills/capability of the spending team in effectively monitoring and scrutinising your department?

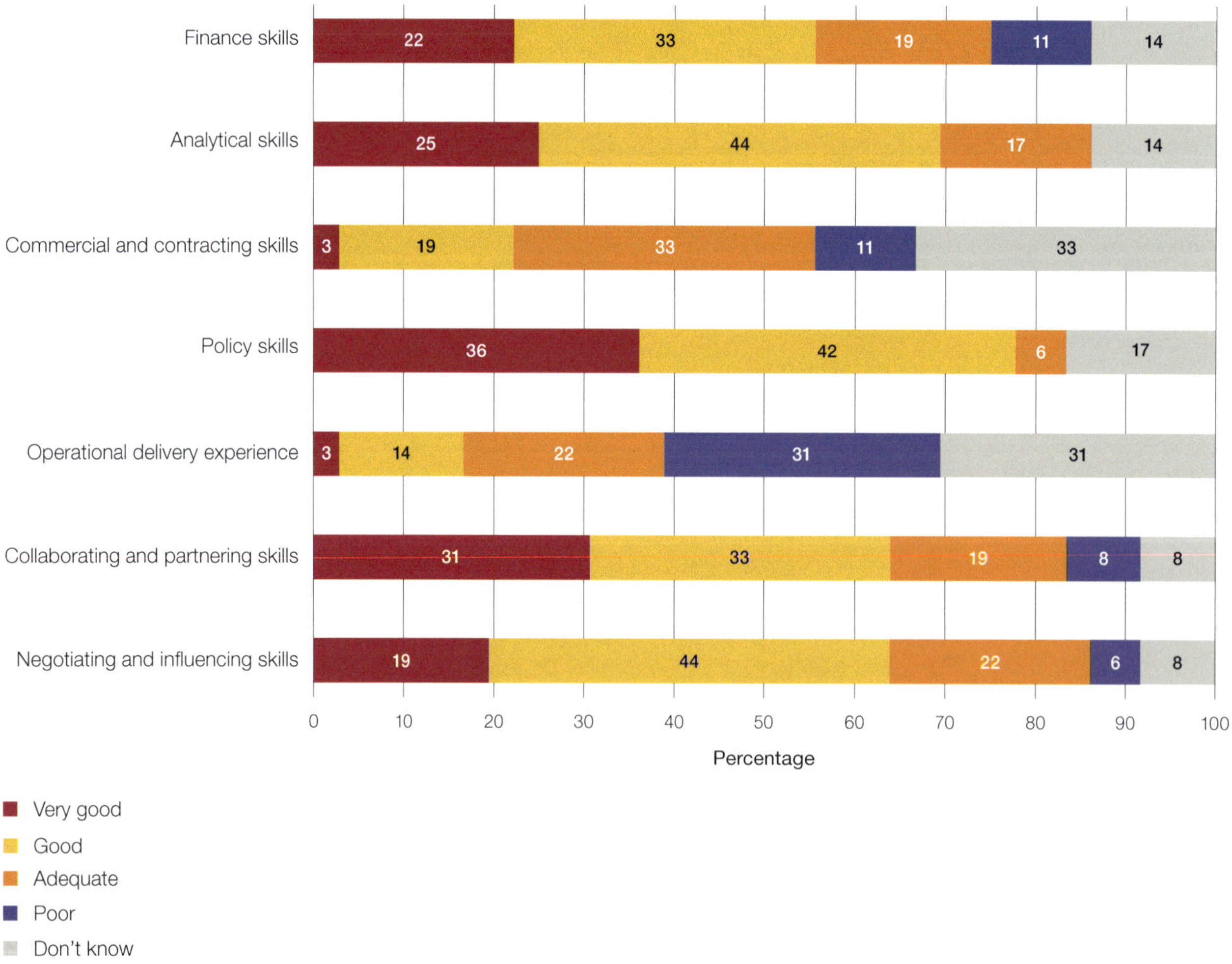

Note
1 Percentages may not add up to exactly 100 due to rounding.

Source: National Audit Office survey of 35 to 36 staff across departments who have direct contact with their department's spending team

3.10 Respondents who expressed a view said that they would like to see junior staff improve on: getting a grasp of wider government issues; understanding departmental pressures; and experience in financial management and cross-government challenges rather than theory. We noted that junior staff have been seconded from some departments to spending teams to provide background and in-depth knowledge of those departments.

3.11 In 2017-18, staff turnover in HM Treasury overall was 21%. More junior staff, who are responsible for much of the day-to-day interaction between spending teams and departments, represent 93% of spending team staff. The median time that these staff had been in their current post, as at March 2018, was eleven months, although HM Treasury data show that the median time they had been working in HM Treasury was just over two years and the civil service was just over three years. Some departments we spoke to highlighted the negative impact of turnover, and 22% of survey respondents said that their department was affected by turnover in their spending team. Three respondents said it affected the spending team's overall understanding of their business and ability to get through business-as-usual activity promptly. HM Treasury said that its policy is for spending team staff to change role every 18 months to three years, depending on seniority. It recognises the risk that high staff turnover creates in maintaining skills and experience. More stability among senior staff can mitigate some of these risks. As at 31 March 2018, HM Treasury's data show that the median time that senior staff (deputy director level) had been in their current HM Treasury post was 14 months but the median time they had been working in HM Treasury was just over 4 years and the civil service was just over 14 years.

3.12 HM Treasury told us that each spending team has a knowledge manager to help make sure knowledge is retained despite turnover. We observed that comprehensive handover notes were prepared for incoming staff on the Ministry of Housing, Communities & Local Government team, for example. HM Treasury has also improved training in response to our 2016 report. Rather than one week of general training, new staff now have three weeks of formal induction, covering core HM Treasury guidance and issues to look at when considering policy proposals, resource implications and financial management information. Training thereafter is 70% on the job, 20% through coaching and 10% through formal courses. Spending team staff can attend further training on spending and finance as appropriate.

3.13 The most significant change since our 2016 report is that the spending teams now explicitly rely on functional experts in other parts of the centre of government (paragraph 1.13 and Figure 5). For example, spending teams bring in the Infrastructure and Projects Authority (IPA) when reviewing departments' project and programme business cases, or to sit on project boards (see Figure 2). HM Treasury also draws on the Government Commercial Function, and the Government Digital Service on digital, data and technology.

3.14 There are some examples of spending teams using new sources of information to gain greater insight into departments' issues. For example:

- HM Treasury told us that the costing projects have provided insight into some significant areas of spending (paragraph 1.10); and
- HM Treasury's Planning and Performance Team has briefed spending teams on single departmental plans (SDPs), and spending teams have provided input on the measures and content set out in them. The HM Treasury Cabinet Office spending team was routinely using the SDP in its discussions with the Cabinet Office.

3.15 However, we found:

- around one-half of survey respondents disagreed or did not know whether spending teams drew insight from initiatives such as costing projects or value maps; and
- no evidence that the other three of the four spending teams we examined were routinely using SDPs. In interviews with departments we noted that spending teams do not routinely refer to measures set out in SDPs when assessing departments' performance. Similarly, 52% of survey respondents did not agree or did not know if spending teams referred to SDPs when making funding decisions (**Figure 22**).

Spending teams' monitoring of departments

3.16 A key part of spending teams' role is scrutinising departments' funding bids on projects and programmes which exceed delegated limits (paragraph 3.8) or where the work is novel or contentious. HM Treasury challenge is a key control. Spending teams scrutinise proposals on deliverability and value-for-money grounds, drawing on the expertise of the government functions (Figure 5). Some 84% of survey respondents agreed that HM Treasury challenges the value for money of funding bids (Figure 22). Spending teams review and challenge written business cases at formal approval points and for the largest and most complex major projects, HM Treasury and the IPA's Major Projects Review Group (MPRG) will convene a panel to consider deliverability, affordability and value for money. The MPRG is co-chaired by the chief executive of the civil service and the director general for public spending. It is supported by external experts and senior civil servants, such as the chief executive of the IPA and the government chief commercial officer.

Figure 22
Officials' views of the day-to-day monitoring provided by spending teams

To what extent do you agree or disagree with the following statements about the day-to-day activities of the spending team? The spending team:

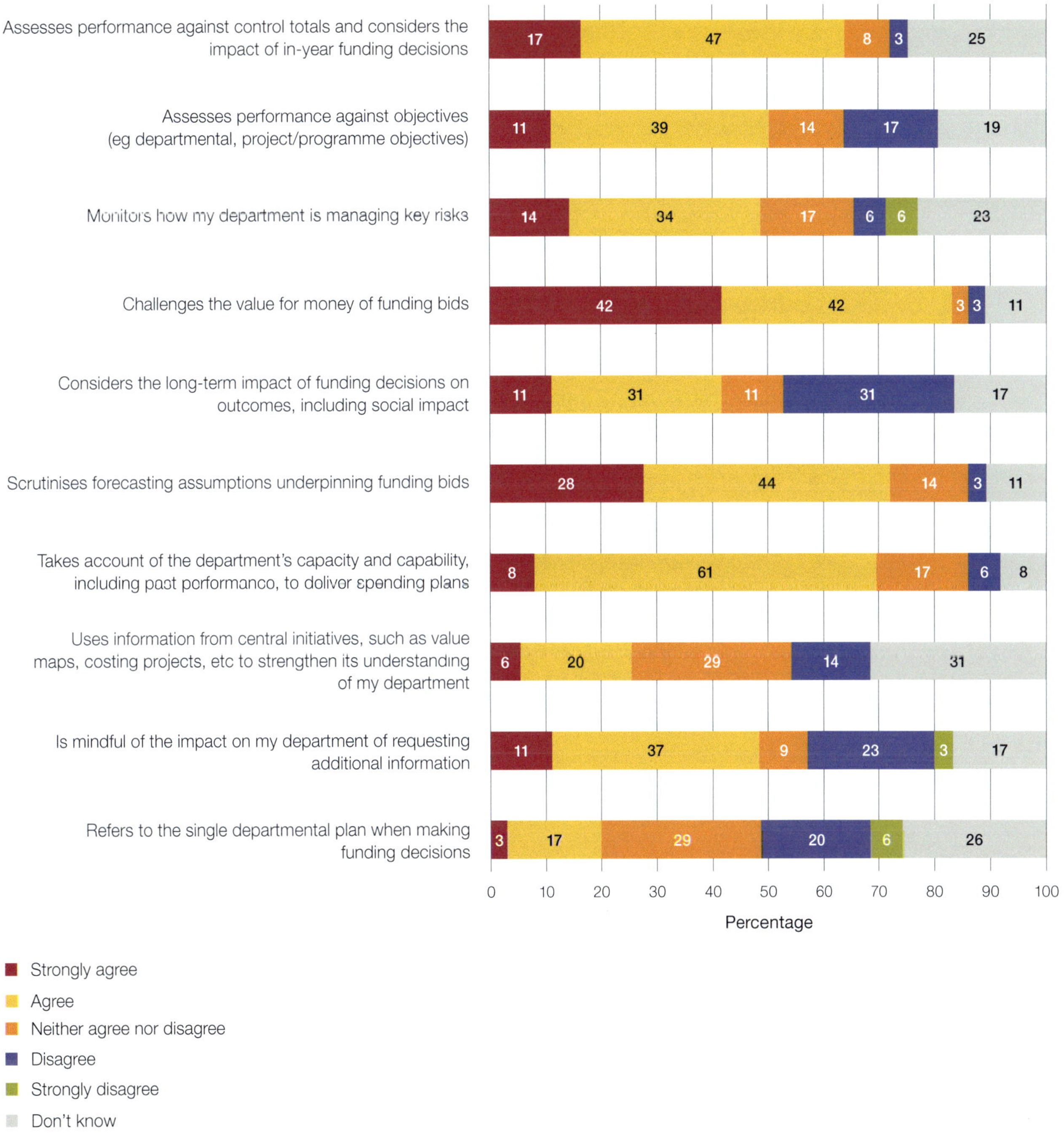

Note

1 Percentages may not add up to exactly 100 due to rounding.

Source: National Audit Office survey of 35 to 36 staff across departments who have direct contact with their department's spending team

3.17 HM Treasury approves projects subject to a set of formal conditions that the department's Accounting Officer is required to meet. HM Treasury noted that it was the IPA's role to assess project performance and it would feed in this information and highlight any concerns to spending teams. The IPA covers the portfolio of major projects and programmes but not all business cases requiring HM Treasury approval. The IPA said it had work under way to assess benefits delivered from major projects to provide a long-term view, and that it aimed in future to provide benchmarking data to spending teams. The IPA and HM Treasury have sought to raise awareness of benefits realisation across government and place greater emphasis on building monitoring into projects throughout their lifecycle. However, there remain inconsistencies in departments' monitoring and evaluation of projects and their outcomes and reporting on benefits is variable and not published.[52]

3.18 Spending teams do not routinely monitor performance against an agreed set of objectives or conditions. Instead, as reflected by survey responses (Figure 22) and our discussions with departments, monthly monitoring focuses on financial performance. HM Treasury told us that it was not its role to 'police' departments' compliance with conditions or delivery of objectives and that the teams were not resourced to do significant follow-up. We found variation in spending teams' approach to tracking projects and programmes after approval. For example:

- spending teams told us that they would check compliance with conditions the next time a business case came in;
- in some instances, monitoring would be carried out by the Cabinet Office Implementation Unit;
- in others, spending teams would monitor progress on high-risk projects or programmes, such as nuclear, post-approval; and
- another spending team had been discussing with the relevant department how to monitor implementation of conditions.

52 Comptroller and Auditor General, *Projects leaving the Government's Major Projects Portfolio*, Session 2017–2019, HC 1620, National Audit Office, October 2018.

Part Four

The challenges for Spending Review 2019 and beyond

4.1 The 2019 Spending Review will be an important test of the improvements the Cabinet Office and HM Treasury have made, and how far these have gone towards creating a framework that balances short-term spending control and achievement of long-term value for money. To be effective, the planning and spending framework needs to be able to counteract some perennial problems we observe in government. This part considers the current incentives to:

- prioritise value for money;
- ensure value for money in major projects;
- plan and manage work to meet cross-government objectives in a way that cuts across departmental silos; and
- make realistic plans with real priorities.

It also considers the importance of transparency and the approach to the next Spending Review.

Incentives to prioritise value for money

4.2 HM Treasury is responsible for administering public money. It must balance fiscal objectives with the objectives of delivering value for money now and over the long term. In the years following the financial crisis, reducing debt was the government's priority, and HM Treasury measured its performance using fiscal measures such as public sector net debt and public sector net borrowing. However, following the removal of Public Service Agreements (PSAs) in 2010 there was no counterbalancing set of objectives and measures of the value delivered for public spending.[53]

53 In 1998, the then Government introduced a framework of PSAs as the primary means to set its key, top priority objectives and measure performance against them. Departments and HM Treasury agreed PSAs as part of the spending review process. In return for funding, departments agreed to deliver key outcomes such as reducing child poverty, tackling climate change, and improving healthcare.

4.3 Using only a small set of fiscal and spending control measures creates incentives to prioritise the short term, and can undermine value-for-money considerations. For example, although the government has said that it will explore asset sales where value for money can be secured,[54] its fiscal performance measures could encourage it to sell assets, regardless of any loss made, because of the positive impact on public sector net debt.[55] The Institute for Fiscal Studies recently concluded that the focus on particular measures of public spending had created perverse incentives to keep spending 'off the books' by using private finance initiatives (PFI) and other methods.[56] One department told us that its HM Treasury spending team tends to focus on the short term, and there have been occasions where decisions were less focused on value for money and more concerned with hitting fiscal targets (**Figure 23**).

4.4 HM Treasury recognises that it needs to do more to assess the value being delivered from spending (paragraph 1.11). It has explicitly reflected a commitment to ensuring value for money and improving outcomes in its own strategic objectives for 2018-19. In July 2018, the government announced plans to improve transparency by disclosing to Parliament the impact of asset sales on a variety of fiscal metrics.[57] In the 2018 Autumn Budget, it stated that it would no longer use PFI for new projects, having concluded that it was inflexible and overly complex.[58]

4.5 Our survey showed 84% of officials agreed that spending teams challenged the value for money of funding bids and HM Treasury pointed to recent examples where it prioritised value for money over immediate fiscal benefit. However, HM Treasury has no performance measures other than the well-established fiscal measures of public sector net debt and public sector net borrowing, which do not assess value for money.[59] We also found little reference to value for money in the key internal priorities that are set out in HM Treasury's Single Departmental Plan (SDP), or in the objectives or job descriptions for spending team staff. By comparison, spending control features strongly in individuals' objectives, particularly at more junior levels.

Incentives to ensure value for money in major projects

4.6 HM Treasury told us that, when reviewing business cases for projects and programmes, it drives value for money by applying the principles of the *Green Book* (HM Treasury's manual for evaluating and appraising policy, project and programme proposals).[60] It updated the *Green Book* in 2018 to: emphasise more strongly the need to consider value for money when short-listing options, and the role of evaluation and monitoring throughout project lifecycles; improve guidance on optimism bias, risk and uncertainty, and provide more detailed guidance on cost–benefit analysis.

54 HM Treasury, Budget 2018, HC 1629, 29 October 2018.
55 Comptroller and Auditor General, *Evaluating the government balance sheet: financial assets and investments*, Session 2016-17, HC 463, National Audit Office, June 2016.
56 Institute for Fiscal Studies, *The planning and control of UK public expenditure 1993–2015*, July 2018, available at: www.ifs.org.uk/publications/13155
57 HM Treasury, *Managing Fiscal Risks: government response to the 2017 Fiscal Risks report*, Cm 9647, July 2018.
58 HM Treasury, *Budget 2018*, HC 1629, 29 October 2018.
59 HM Treasury, *HM Treasury Single Departmental Plan*, May 2018, available at: www.gov.uk/government/publications/hm-treasury-single-departmental-plan/hm-treasury-single-departmental-plan--2
60 HM Treasury, *The Green Book – Central Government Guidance on Appraisal and Evaluation*, 2018.

Figure 23

Trade-offs between spending control, fiscal measures and value for money: examples

Reports	Findings
Committee of Public Accounts' report on Private Finance Initiatives (PFI), June 2018[1]	To keep Private Finance 2 off balance sheet, HM Treasury reduced the amount that the public sector will receive from savings made by the private finance companies. More than 25 years on, HM Treasury still has no data on benefits to show whether the PFI model provides value for money.
National Audit Office (NAO) report on the sale of student loans, July 2018[2]	In terms of the preparation, process and proceeds of the transaction itself UKGI has achieved value for money. But the sale of student loans also shows limitations in the way that government assesses value for money and measures the costs of student loans over time. The Department for Education uses one set of assumptions for the cost of student loans when they are added to government's balance sheet, and HM Treasury uses another set of assumptions in support of its decision to sell them. This offers two different ways of calculating the subsidy to, and value of, its rapidly growing student loan portfolio. The two approaches give different answers, which risks government: not knowing with enough certainty the cost to the taxpayer of student loans when they are issued; and of selling assets too cheaply relative to their long-term value despite achieving its objective of reducing public sector net debt.
NAO investigation into the cancellation of three rail electrification projects, March 2018[3]	The Department for Transport and Network Rail proposed addressing a £2.5 billion shortfall in the affordability of Network Rail's project portfolio, by selling around £1.8 billion of Network Rail assets. HM Treasury stipulated that these asset sales would need to reduce public sector net borrowing. This means the structure of the asset sales would need to meet certain financial accounting and reporting requirements. As this was not possible, the Department, Network Rail and HM Treasury decided that they would instead need to cancel projects. Ministers have said the significant journey time savings from the three electrification projects are possible without full electrification, using bi-mode trains supported by advances in technology. However, when we reported in March 2018 it was too early to tell whether the benefits of the original projects could be fully delivered through this revised strategy.
NAO report on Hinkley Point C, June 2017[4]	HM Treasury reviewed the deal during negotiations and emphasised different considerations at various times. In 2013, it considered the deal's potential value for money and noted that it appeared expensive, particularly compared with gas-fired power stations. In its September 2015 review, HM Treasury primarily considered the risk that the deal could mean Hinkley Point C coming onto government's balance sheet. In September 2016, HM Treasury highlighted how the value-for-money case for Hinkley Point C had weakened. But it concluded that the legal, reputational, investor and diplomatic ramifications of not proceeding meant it was, on balance, better to continue with the deal.

Notes

1 HC Committee of Public Accounts, *Private finance initiatives*, Forty-sixth Report of Session 2017–2019, HC 894, June 2018.

2 Comptroller and Auditor General, *The sale of student loans*, Session 2017–2019, HC 1385, National Audit Office, July 2018.

3 Comptroller and Auditor General, *Investigation into the Department for Transport's decision to cancel three rail electrification projects*, Session 2017–2019, HC 835, National Audit Office, March 2018.

4 Comptroller and Auditor General, *Hinkley Point C*, Session 2017-18, HC 40, National Audit Office, June 2017.

Source: National Audit Office

4.7 HM Treasury's processes are not designed to follow up on whether departments have delivered on the commitments set out in business cases and are delivering the promised value or outcomes. HM Treasury told us that it examines the delivery of these commitments when another business case comes in, and at spending reviews, with input from the Infrastructure and Projects Authority (IPA). We found variable tracking of business case commitments by spending teams (paragraph 3.18). The IPA monitors whether benefits are being delivered for projects on the governments' major project portfolio (paragraphs 3.16–3.17). Departments we spoke to said that HM Treasury did not focus on value for money as part of their routine monitoring of departmental performance. Our analysis of risk registers maintained by spending teams showed they focus on spending risks rather than value for money, and there was limited reference to the risk of not delivering the expected outcomes or benefits.

Incentives to plan and manage performance across departmental silos

4.8 Many of government's objectives cut across more than one department and involve services being provided by multiple public bodies, but in 2016 the Committee of Public Accounts said that it saw too little joined-up planning across government.[61] Our recent work shows how government remains weak at planning and managing delivery when it cuts across organisations (**Figure 24**).

4.9 Government has various arrangements to identify and discuss cross-cutting issues:

- Cabinet-level implementation taskforces bring together ministers from across different areas of government to track the implementation of policies on issues that government considers a priority, ranging from housing to modern slavery, and to remove barriers to progress.[62] They are supported by the Cabinet Office's Implementation Unit;
- HM Treasury has established internal groups and work streams to focus on important cross-government issues including productivity and the ageing population; and
- HM Treasury's costings projects have provided an opportunity to look at issues which cut across a number of departments in more depth. Cross-department steering group boards have been established to consider the projects and make recommendations for improvement.

61 HC Committee of Public Accounts, *Managing government spending and performance*, Twenty-seventh Report of Session 2016-17, HC 710, November 2016.

62 There are currently seven implementation taskforces: Digital, Employment and Skills; Housing; Immigration; Industrial Strategy; Rough Sleeping and Homelessness Reduction; Tackling Modern Slavery; and People Trafficking, available at: www.gov.uk/government/publications/the-cabinet-committees-system-and-list-of-cabinet-committees

Figure 24

Planning and managing objectives that cut across government: examples

Managing the Official Development Assistance target, July 2017[1]	The UK Aid Strategy was jointly produced by the Department for International Development (DFID) and HM Treasury. The strategy did not identify which part of government – either on its own or jointly – is responsible for implementing the strategy or for checking on its progress, or is ultimately accountable for its delivery. HM Treasury and DFID co-chair a Senior Officials Group that supports the management and delivery of the ODA target; and DFID and HM Treasury monitor the Official Development Assistance expenditure of other government departments and funds. Each department has a responsibility to make sure all of its expenditure, including Official Development Assistance, secures value for money. However, in 2017 we found that no single part of government was responsible for monitoring the overall effectiveness and coherence of spending on Official Development Assistance.
Financial sustainability of local authorities 2018, March 2018[2]	There is no single point within government that monitors the impact of funding reductions across the full range of local authority services on an ongoing basis. Departments tend to have an understanding of their service area at the local level, but not necessarily of the potential implications of pressures in other service areas. A consequence is that the integrated nature of service delivery in local authorities, in which the sustainability of individual services is often shaped by decisions and pressures in other services, is not reflected at the departmental level.
Local support for people with a learning disability, March 2017[3]	People with a learning disability need a range of support from different areas of government, such as with welfare benefits and human rights. Despite this, the Department of Health & Social Care, which has the strategic lead for adult learning disability support, has no current cross-government strategy for the learning disability population. In 2009, it published a strategy called *Valuing People Now,* which ran for three years and had not been replaced by the time we reported in 2017.
Improving children and young people's mental health services, October 2018[4]	The government does not have cross-government accountability arrangements in place to ensure Future in Mind is delivered as intended. The government has formed an inter-ministerial group, and supporting cross-departmental group, to discuss mental health policy and share information. There are individual programme governance arrangements in place for the Forward View and cross-sector arrangements starting for the green paper. However, as the government is not managing Future in Mind as a single programme of work, there is no single governance structure for its delivery.
Homelessness, September 2017[5]	The Ministry of Housing, Communities and Local Government has overarching objectives for preventing and addressing homelessness. It has agreed outcomes for specific programmes with local authorities. It also works with other departments with an interest: including the Department of Health, Ministry of Justice, Department for Work & Pensions, and Home Office. The Ministry of Housing, Communities and Local Government believes it is taking a strategic approach to homelessness reduction. However, when we reported in September 2017 it had not published an overarching strategy setting out the overall reduction in homelessness that it wants to achieve through its spending and activities, or the contribution to this that it plans to deliver through its different programmes and the work of other departments. It had also not fully assessed the impact of government's welfare reforms on homelessness.

Notes

1 Comptroller and Auditor General, *Managing the Official Development Assistance target – a report on progress*, Session 2017–2019, HC 243, National Audit Office, July 2017.

2 Comptroller and Auditor General, *Financial sustainability of local authorities 2018*, Session 2017–2019, HC 834, National Audit Office, March 2018.

3 Comptroller and Auditor General, *Local support for people with a learning disability*, Session 2016-17, HC 1053, National Audit Office, March 2017.

4 Comptroller and Auditor General, *Improving children and young people's mental health services,* Session 2017–2019, HC 1618, National Audit Office, October 2018.

5 Comptroller and Auditor General, *Homelessness*, Session 2017–2019, HC 308, National Audit Office, September 2017.

Source: National Audit Office

4.10 The Cabinet Office and HM Treasury have prompted some departments to make links with others (**Figure 25**), and there are cross-government networks at which departments can discuss finance and business planning. The guidance to departments on SDPs also requires them to report on contributions to cross-government objectives.[63] Departments we spoke to also said that spending teams had applied their strategic perspective to help departments make links to other related activity, which was backed up by 54% of survey respondents. But our discussions with departments suggest they do not routinely share their SDPs across government. And ultimately, as our survey confirms, there are limited *formal* mechanisms or incentives for departments to join up business planning or funding bids (Figure 25). HM Treasury told us it is trying to encourage cross-departmental bids and will consider how best to allow for this in the next spending review.

Figure 25

How well spending teams support cross-cutting objectives

To what extent do you agree with the following statements? The spending team:

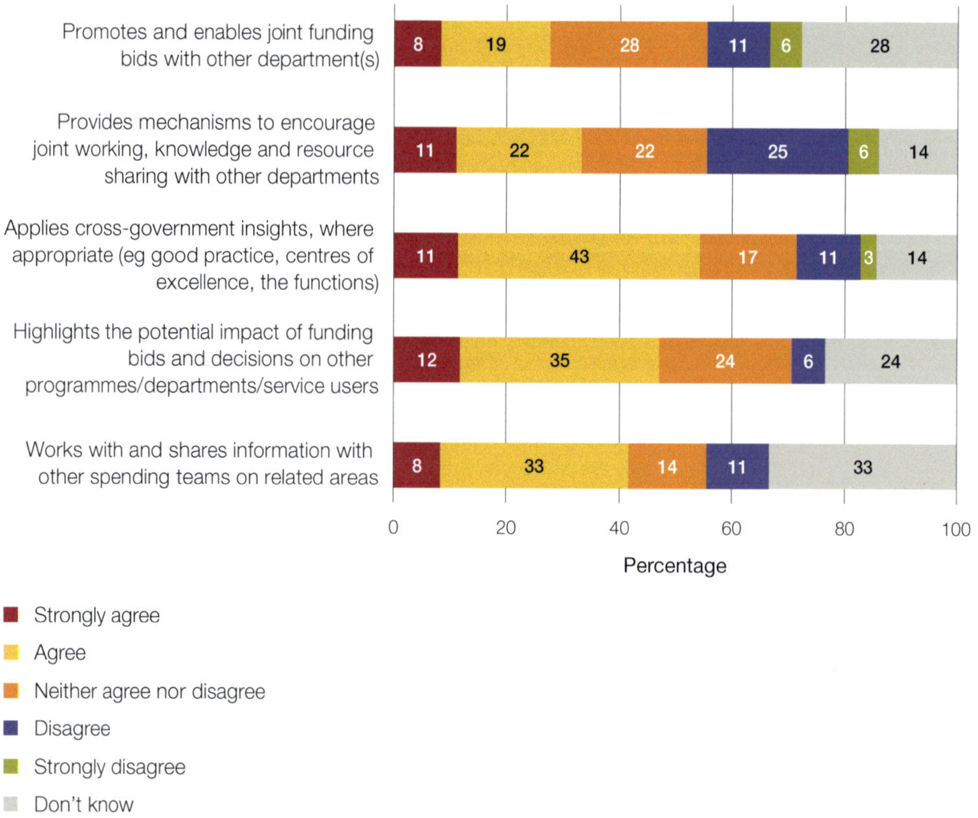

Note

1 Percentages may not add up to exactly 100 due to rounding.

Source: National Audit Office survey of staff across departments who have direct contact with their department's spending team

63 Specifically, departments are asked to include in their SDPs how they are contributing to: the Strategic Defence and Security Review, the Housing White Paper, the Sustainability and Development Goals, Overseas Development Assistance, Greening Government commitments, government's digital transformation strategy, and Rural Proofing.

4.11 There is also a lack of visibility of performance on cross-cutting issues:

- *The Government's Plan*, published in December 2017, was the first time that the government had set out a single set of priorities based upon the public SDPs. It has seven high-level objectives and 20 items listed under 'how we will achieve this', but they are a mixture of vision statements, inputs, milestones and outputs, with no performance metrics or data.[64]

- Implementation taskforces do not publish plans or progress. In 2016 the Committee of Public Accounts recommended that government should regularly report on how the taskforces are improving delivery, but government did not agree, saying, "While Implementation taskforces perform a vital role in the delivery of the government's cross-cutting priorities, they... operate in a complex delivery environment meaning it may not be possible to attribute specific improvements to their activity."[65,66] To see what government is doing on each taskforce area, the reader would need to look through all 18 public plans and pick out relevant measures. Cabinet Office told us that the taskforces are looking at whether their metrics are aligned with those in the SDPs.

Incentives to make realistic plans with real priorities

4.12 Government has a record of over-programming, dating to well before the decision to leave the EU. In 2014 the civil service chief executive said, "We are doing 30% too much across the board, we always have been."[67] Optimism bias remains a problem in major projects.[68] However, it is increasingly well-understood, and accounting officers are now required to give positive, public assurance that each major project is feasible and affordable.[69] As regards the overall feasibility and affordability of the whole SDP, however, there is no such formal control, despite the fact that accounting officers are required to plan on an affordable and sustainable path, within their agreed spending limits and in a way that delivers good value for the Exchequer as a whole.[70] Unwillingness to make politically difficult prioritisation decisions – to match plans to available resources – is an entrenched issue. Our work in 2018 confirms that SDPs are not yet providing robust enough evidence to counteract this tendency (paragraph 2.14).

64 Cabinet Office, *Building a country that works for everyone: the government's plan*, December 2017, available at: www.gov.uk/government/collections/a-country-that-works-for-everyone-the-governments-plan
65 HC Committee of Public Accounts, *Managing government spending and performance*, Twenty-seventh Report of Session 2016-17, HC 710, November 2016.
66 HM Treasury, *Treasury Minutes: Government responses to the Committee of Public Accounts on the Twenty-sixth, the Twenty-seventh and the Twenty-ninth to the Thirty-fourth Reports from Session 2016-17*, Cm 9429, March 2017.
67 HC Committee of Public Accounts, *Oral evidence: The work of the Chief Executive of the Civil Service*, HC 806, November 2014, available at: http://data.parliament.uk/writtenevidence/committeeevidence.svc/evidencedocument/public-accounts-committee/the-work-of-the-chief-executive-of-the-civil-service/oral/15823.pdf
68 Examples include those described at: Comptroller and Auditor General, *Department for Transport and Network Rail, Modernising the Great Western railway*, Session 2016-17, HC 781, National Audit Office, November 2016; and Comptroller and Auditor General, HM Revenue & Customs, *HM Revenue & Customs Annual Reports and Accounts 2015-16*, HC 338, National Audit Office, July 2016.
69 See Accounting Officer Assessments guidance at www.gov.uk/government/publications/accounting-officer-assessments
70 HM Treasury, *Managing Public Money*, published July 2013 with annexes revised as at March 2018.

4.13 Recent spending reviews have been characterised by bilateral deal-making between departments and HM Treasury, and incentives to meet short-term spending targets.[71] Funding agreements between HM Treasury and departments have not been balanced by a commitment to deliver an agreed level of performance (except in a narrow financial sense and for selected projects). This creates a risk that departments and HM Treasury are complicit in agreeing over-optimistic delivery or spending reduction plans that have no realistic chance of being delivered. Departments have their short-term funding needs met; and HM Treasury gets the savings it needs to meet its fiscal targets. Performance problems that begin to appear can be patched up with short-term funding boosts, when the fiscal position makes this possible.[72] Meanwhile the long-standing lack of transparency around performance and value for money has made it extremely difficult for Parliament or citizens to hold government to account for failure to deliver.

Approach to the next Spending Review

4.14 In March 2018, the Chancellor of the Exchequer announced that there would be a Spending Review in 2019. The 2018 Autumn Budget has set out an indicative 5-year path for departmental resource spending, but the final envelope for Spending Review 2019 will be set out in due course.[73] This Spending Review has the potential to be the most challenging in recent times. Ministers and senior public servants have been reported as calling for budget increases after years of austerity[74] and there is significant uncertainty about the fiscal impact of leaving the European Union.[75] Although the design of the Spending Review is still being agreed, departments were asked to identify potential savings well in advance.

71 Comptroller and Auditor General, *Spending Review 2015*, Session 2016-17, HC 571, National Audit Office, July 2016.

72 Comptroller and Auditor General, Ministry of Housing, Communities & Local Government, *Financial sustainability of local authorities 2018*, Session 2017–2019, HC 834, National Audit Office, March 2018; Comptroller and Auditor General, Department of Health & Social Care, *Sustainability and transformation in the NHS*, Session 2017–2019, HC 719, National Audit Office, January 2018; Comptroller and Auditor General, *Financial sustainability of police forces in England and Wales 2018*, Session 2017–2019, HC 1501, National Audit Office, September 2018.

73 HM Treasury and The Rt Hon Philip Hammond MP, *Spring Statement 2018: Philip Hammond's speech*, 13 March 2018, available at: www.gov.uk/government/speeches/spring-statement-2018-philip-hammonds-speech

74 For example: D Haynes and F Elliott, 'Billions more needed for defence, says Gavin Williamson', *The Times*, 27 June 2018, available at www.thetimes.co.uk; G Heffer, 'Sajid Javid admits police do not have enough resources as he faces pay anger', *Sky News*, 11 September 2018; P Butler, 'Not enough money to run vital services, warn England's councils', *The Guardian*, 20 September 2018.

75 HM Treasury, *Managing fiscal risks: government response to the 2017 Fiscal risks report*, Cm 9647, July 2018.

4.15 The Chief Secretary to the Treasury has said she wants to drive better value for money through a "zero-based, zero-tolerance approach to wasteful spend".[76] And she has called for a "new relationship between HM Treasury and departments … to give our leaders the freedom to lead, encourage creativity and innovation whilst holding them to account for their performance".[77] At Budget 2018, HM Treasury stated that it would build on experience and lessons learned and that the Spending Review 2019 will aim to ensure that performance and outcomes achieved for the money invested in public services are tracked systematically.[78]

4.16 Departments too would like to see change – a number took the initiative and began asking spending teams about preparations for the Spending Review as early as February 2018. Senior departmental staff answering our survey said they would like to see:

- early clarification, and open conversations about the Spending Review process;
- a focus on high-level strategic objectives, not micro details or policy initiatives;
- alignment with the business planning process; and
- the centre of government specifically ensuring that performance measures are aligned and do not encourage 'problem shifting'.

4.17 It still remains very difficult for the public and Parliament to see and scrutinise the choices government is making. Government does not publish the details of how decisions and trade-offs in spending reviews are made. Public plans contain only high-level summary information on activities and performance, and none on changes in spending. Neither do public plans include information on changing priorities – departments set out 9% more objectives and sub-objectives in 2018 (389) than in 2017 (358), but do not set out how they are prioritising between the competing demands on their resources, or what has been stopped. Several parliamentary committees have called for greater visibility of aspects of government's spending plans and performance.[79]

76 HM Treasury and The Rt Hon Elizabeth Truss MP, *Chief Secretary to the Treasury Liz Truss speech to the London School of Economics*, 26 June 2018, available at: www.gov.uk/government/speeches/chief-secretary-to-the-treasury-liz-truss-speech-to-the-london-school-of-economics

77 HM Treasury, *Delivering better outcomes for citizens: practical steps for unlocking public value*, led by Sir Michael Barber, November 2017.

78 HM Treasury, *Budget 2018,* HC 1629, October 2018.

79 In addition to the work of the Committee of Public Accounts, see: Public Administration and Constitutional Affairs Committee, *Accounting for democracy: making sure Parliament, the people and ministers know how and why public money is spent*, Session 2016-17, HC 95, April 2017; and House of Commons Procedure Committee, *Authorising Government expenditure: steps to more effective scrutiny*, Session 2016-17, HC 190, March 2017.

4.18 The centre of government, departments and the functions are beginning to share information ahead of the Spending Review, and HM Treasury is working with the Cabinet Office on how to use the information in SDPs to inform the Spending Review. It remains to be seen whether government will use these additional insights to have an honest and open discussion about priorities, allocations and the implications for public services, such as police and local government, which are already under financial pressure.[80] Departments are well used to the way spending reviews are traditionally conducted and are already drawing up their negotiating positions. Should departments perceive that their efforts on business planning have no effect on funding allocations, they may feel no incentive to continue improving.

80 Comptroller and Auditor General, *Financial sustainability of police forces in England and Wales 2018*, Session 2017–2019, HC 1501, National Audit Office, September 2018; Comptroller and Auditor General, Department for Work & Pensions, *Rolling out Universal Credit*, Session 2017–2019, HC 1123, National Audit Office, June 2018; Comptroller and Auditor General, *Financial sustainability of local authorities 2018*, Session 2017–2019, HC 834, National Audit Office, March 2018.

Appendix One

Our audit approach

1 This study examined the progress made by Cabinet Office and HM Treasury in improving the government's planning and spending framework since we last reported in 2016. We reviewed current business planning arrangements and the work of HM Treasury's spending teams to conclude on:

- the effectiveness of business planning in government;
- the challenges of planning in the government environment;
- developments since 2016 to improve planning;
- the role of HM Treasury spending teams in financial decision-making;
- spending teams' skills and capabilities and the dynamic between them and departments; and
- preparedness for the next Spending Review.

2 This report began as two separate value-for-money studies, one on business planning and one on the role of HM Treasury spending teams. In view of the strong links between planning and spending decisions, and the complementary roles of the Cabinet Office and HM Treasury in this area, we decided to amalgamate the two and publish one report. This allowed us to combine related findings and present a holistic view of the opportunities to for improvement.

3 **Figure 26** on pages 66 and 67 gives our evaluative criteria. Our evidence base is described in Appendix Two.

Figure 26
Our audit approach

Business planning framework study

The objective of government

The Cabinet Office supports and monitors the implementation of government's policies and the Prime Minister's priorities.

How this will be achieved

The Cabinet Office is responsible for overseeing departments' business planning: how departments set priorities, plan activity, allocate money and monitor progress and performance.

Our study

The study examined whether business planning has improved since 2016, and examined the remaining challenges to improving business planning.

Our evaluative criteria

Has the Cabinet Office improved the standard of business planning across government?

Is government's current approach to planning and prioritisation effective?

Is there scope for government to improve the planning framework and planning practice across government?

Our evidence (see Appendix Two for details)

- We interviewed officials in the Cabinet Office and other government departments.
- We surveyed people working on business planning in government departments about their experience of planning and working with spending teams.
- We reviewed documents including departments' single departmental plans (SDPs) and the Cabinet Office's assessment of the quality of draft plans.

Our conclusions

HM Treasury has, these many years, demonstrated that it is highly effective at controlling public spending. It has, relatively recently, turned its focus towards a renewed drive to improve value for money. There have been positive developments in this direction, not least the Barber review, the provision of specialist advisers to the spending teams and more. Likewise, the Cabinet Office has been working to improve the maturity of business planning across departments.

However, there are occasions when we see value for money being compromised by the needs of short-term spending control. Unrealistic, over-optimistic budgets are kept within the spending envelope by short-term unplanned cuts, which can damage long-term programmes and drive suppliers to distraction.

All this turbulence can only be minimised by integrated medium- and short-term planning activity, strongly policed and challenged for realism and deliverability by the HM Treasury spending teams, and supported by the Cabinet Office and the civil service functions. This may require different skills and a significant change in mind-set both at the centre of government and in departments. Without these changes, government will continue to be trapped in a cycle of short-termism, over-optimism and silo decision-making, which creates real risks to value for money.

Spending framework study

The objective of government

HM Treasury has overall responsibility, and sets the rules, for the administration of public money, and delegates funding to accounting officers who lead spending departments. It has a strategic objective to place the public finances on a sustainable footing, ensuring value for money and improved outcomes in public services.

How this will be achieved

The centre of government manages government's finances by directing, monitoring and controlling resources, through small teams that work with each government department.

Our study

The study examined the spending teams' role, the dynamic between spending teams and departments and HM Treasury's preparedness for the next spending review.

Our evaluative criteria

- How is the operating model for spending teams organised to support effective challenge?
- How do spending teams inform themselves to be able to effectively challenge departments?
- How well prepared are spending teams for the next spending review?

Our evidence (see Appendix Two for details)

- We interviewed officials in HM Treasury and other government departments.
- We surveyed people working in government departments about their experience of working with spending teams.
- We reviewed documents including guidance and training material, risk registers, meeting minutes, objectives and job descriptions and business cases.
- We analysed spending team staff data.

Appendix Two

Our evidence base

1 Our conclusion was reached following an analysis of evidence collected between April and September 2018. Our main methods are outlined below.

Document review

2 We reviewed key documents including:

- government departments' single departmental plans (SDPs) and supporting documents;
- public SDPs;
- policy documents and guidance for departments;
- Cabinet Office's analysis of and feedback to departments on their draft SDPs;
- HM Treasury spending team organisation charts, and examples of job descriptions and individuals' objectives;
- spending teams' risk registers;
- guidance and training material used by spending teams;
- examples of information used by spending teams including monthly reports from departments and project business cases;
- meeting minutes of senior spending team officials;
- applications from departments to HM Treasury for additional funds to support EU Exit work; and
- evidence and examples from our previous work on: business planning and allocative decision-making, preparations for the UK's exit from the EU, and systemic issues affecting delivery of value for money.

We used this documentary evidence to understand how the planning and spending framework was operated and overseen.

Interviews

3 We conducted semi-structured interviews with officials to understand their view of aspects of the planning and spending framework, practices and progress within departments, and the oversight provided by the centre of government (Cabinet Office and HM Treasury). We also used these interviews to identify relevant documentary evidence. We interviewed officials at HM Treasury, the Cabinet Office, Department of Health & Social Care, Department of Digital, Culture, Media & Sport, Ministry of Defence, Ministry of Justice, Ministry of Housing, Communities & Local Government, Department for Work & Pensions, HM Revenue & Customs, Government Property Agency and the Infrastructure and Projects Authority.

4 We also discussed business planning and allocative decision-making with the Institute of Chartered Accountants in England and Wales, the Chartered Institute of Public Finance and Accountancy and the Institute for Government.

Quantitative analysis

5 We sent an online survey to 164 officials in the 18 main government departments who have direct or indirect involvement in business planning, and/or work with HM Treasury's spending teams. This included finance directors general, finance directors, departmental staff working in finance, corporate or strategy teams, and non-executive directors.

- We received 64 responses in total. This represented a response rate of 55% of finance directors general and directors, 56% of non-executive directors, 39% of the whole survey population, and 34% of other departmental staff.
- The survey took place between May and September 2018.
- We sought views on government's business planning, including the role of the centre of government, and on the particular role of HM Treasury spending teams in financial decision-making.
- The survey included a mixture of closed and open questions. We carried out descriptive analyses of responses. Unless otherwise indicated, we present our results for the whole sample.

6 Separately, we analysed data on spending team staff to understand the length of time in service for each grade.

Appendix Three

Committee of Public Accounts' recommendations and government's response

Figure 27

Committee of Public Accounts' recommendations and government's response

Report – Managing government spending and performance, 2016[1]

Committee of Public Accounts' conclusion	Recommendation
Government has made some progress in the way it plans and manages its business. Government makes plans with a poor understanding of current performance, of the outcomes it is seeking, and of the link between outcomes and associated funding. Many of the government's key objectives cut across more than one department and involve multiple organisations delivering services. The Committee is yet to be convinced that Single Departmental Plans (SDPs) will be able to deal with significant changes in priorities within and beyond this Parliament (for example, Brexit). There is significant variation in the maturity of planning across individual government departments, and no shared approach to encourage continuous improvement. The SDPs do not enable taxpayers or Parliament to understand the government's plans and how it is performing, and therefore have not enhanced their ability to hold the government to account for its spending.[3]	HM Treasury and the Cabinet Office, working together, should now set out a vision of how the overall approach to how government plans and manages its business will ensure value for money across government, and a plan for how they will get to that state at least in time for the next Spending Review. This should include: • how individual processes, including spending reviews and SDPs, will be integrated to improve government's ability to deliver value for money, underpinned by rapid progress with the Financial Management Review; • how both government and taxpayers can use all the different public information (including the Spending Review, SDPs, Annual Reports, and Estimates) as a package, to see what government is planning, how much it is spending, and what it is achieving, against a consistent set of objectives which cover both the implementation of new policies and programmes and 'business as usual'; • how the quality of planning and management in different departments will be brought up to a consistently high standard; and • how the approach can accommodate both the long-term view needed for many government projects and programmes, and the flexibility needed to meet any new administration's shorter-term commitments. HM Treasury and the Cabinet Office should work with departments on practical ways to improve joined-up planning across government, to bring planning and delivery out of the confines of departmental boundaries.
	HM Treasury and the Cabinet Office should regularly report on how the Cabinet implementation taskforces are improving delivery.

Government's response

The government agrees with the Committee's recommendations.[3]

Target implementation date: June 2017.

Single departmental plans (SDPs) establish a consistent framework for medium-term business planning to link what a department will deliver and how a department will deliver it, within the multi-year Spending Review settlement. Plans are refreshed on an annual basis to respond to policy and fiscal announcements and encourage routine consideration of planned delivery and any need for reprioritisation. A central point of review will identify and encourage join-up between departments during the planning process. Published SDPs allow the public to track progress against departmental objectives and a broader report on performance is available in the public domain through annual reports and accounts. The establishment of SDPs is part of HM Treasury and Cabinet Office's overall effort to continuously improve and develop the way government plans and manages its business to deliver value for money.

To make it clearer how this approach supports the government to plan and manage its business and how existing public information can be used, HM Treasury and Cabinet Office intend to set out the government's planning and performance process, alongside the refreshed public SDPs and improved links to the performance information within them.

HM Treasury and Cabinet Office will establish a planning and performance peer group of government departments, aligned with the Financial Management Reform programme. HM Treasury and Cabinet Office will agree, with government departments, the priority activities needed to establish a consistent high standard and deliver continuous improvement to this planning and performance management approach. Both departments will continue to work with the National Audit Office (NAO) to inform this work, which will inform actions taken for the next Spending Review.

The government disagrees with the Committee's recommendation.[3]

Due to longstanding principles of confidentiality for Cabinet committees and equivalent ministerial forums, the government does not comment on the activity of the Implementation Taskforces.

While implementation taskforces perform a vital role in the delivery of the government's cross-cutting priorities, they do not report publicly and they operate in a complex delivery environment, meaning it may not be possible to attribute specific improvements to their activity. Transparent information of progress on policy areas covered by the implementation taskforces are routinely made available through relevant departmental annual reports and accounts or the release of performance information and official statistics.

Figure 27 *continued*

Committee of Public Accounts' recommendations and government's response

Report – Managing government spending and performance, 2016[1] *continued*

Committee of Public Accounts' conclusion	Recommendation
Government has made some progress in the way it plans and manages its business. Government makes plans with a poor understanding of current performance, of the outcomes it is seeking, and of the link between outcomes and associated funding. Many of the government's key objectives cut across more than one department and involve multiple organisations delivering services. The Committee is yet to be convinced that Single Departmental Plans (SDPs) will be able to deal with significant changes in priorities within and beyond this Parliament (for example, Brexit). There is significant variation in the maturity of planning across individual government departments, and no shared approach to encourage continuous improvement. The SDPs do not enable taxpayers or Parliament to understand the government's plans and how it is performing, and therefore have not enhanced their ability to hold the government to account for its spending.[3]	HM Treasury and the Cabinet Office, and all departments, should make sure that SDPs are kept 'live' and are central to any discussions about reprioritisation and related funding decisions. Departments should update published SDPs to reflect recent changes in responsibilities and priorities by the end of the 2016-17 financial year at the latest. For the benefit of both Parliament and the public, departments should publish the same up-to-date information about performance that they use for monitoring themselves, subject to any national security or similar essential restrictions. There should be regular public reporting of government's performance, at least twice yearly, to adequately provide the transparency on performance that was lost when the mid-year reporting to Parliament was dropped.

Government's response

The government agrees with the Committee's recommendation.[3]

Recommendation implemented.

Single departmental plans will be refreshed on an annual basis, in line with the planning cycle for each financial year. All government departments have been requested to refresh and update their SDP for April 2017. The request has been aligned with the Efficiency Review and preparations to leave the European Union (EU) to encourage departments to make assessments on reprioritisation as part of their planning process and to take account of changes in priorities. Departments are encouraged to use their SDPs as the framework for ongoing business planning; and tracking progress and performance. SDPs provide regular reporting to the Cabinet Office.

The government agrees with the Committee's recommendation.[3]

Target implementation date: May 2017.

Departments will update published single departmental plans to reflect recent changes in responsibilities and priorities and improve how departments present how they work together to deliver shared priorities. SDPs will be published at the start of the new financial year to allow departments to reflect the latest fiscal and policy announcements from Spring Budget 2017.

The government agrees with the Committee's recommendation.[3]

The government's aim when publishing performance information is to balance the need for a clear, transparent and comprehensive view of the performance of vital public services with the need for ministers and accounting officers to monitor government performance and manage their own affairs. The NAO's *Government's management of its performance: progress with single departmental plans* report acknowledges that "it is not reasonable to expect the government to share every detail of its plans and progress" and it "recognises the need for a safe space" for minsters to take decisions before options are finalised".

That said, HM Treasury and Cabinet Office consider further improvements can be made and will promote greater access to information in the refreshed, published SDPs by including a schedule of supporting statistics and their frequency. Headline indicators will be updated at least twice a year, or more regularly, when new data become available. Supplementary Estimates and the associated memorandums continue to provide additional information including in-year spending and how the Supplementary Estimate will be applied to achieve departmental objectives. Annual reports and accounts continue to provide a fuller picture of financial and non-financial performance at year end, based on SDP objectives, where relevant.

Further official statistics on performance, public spending and workforce, used by departments to monitor performance, are routinely released into the public domain when they become available. A variety of releases are also issued by the Office for National Statistics (ONS) that cover both economic and non-economic statistics. This includes the monthly 'Public Sector Finances' release that is jointly prepared with HM Treasury. HM Treasury publishes Public Spending Statistics on the GOV.UK website that provides information on departmental spending over the previous five years, which is updated on a quarterly basis. HM Treasury ministers decided, in 2016, that there was no longer any need to ask departments to prepare mid-year reports due to the information already available from these sources.

The government considers that, with these improvements, the right balance is struck between transparency of information and allowing departments a 'safe space' to manage their own affairs. HM Treasury and Cabinet Office will continue to consider where further improvements can be made in future.

Figure 27 *continued*

Committee of Public Accounts' recommendations and government's response

Report – Exiting the European Union, 2018[2]

Recommendation

By March 2018, departments should re-visit their existing commitments to test their realism against likely capacity and resources. Departments should demonstrate in their published single departmental plans, no later than April 2018, how they have resourced the new priorities, including evidence of what has been de-prioritised as a result.

Government's response

The government disagrees with the Committee's recommendation.[4]

Government departments have actively prioritised activity as part of their internal business planning processes for the 2018-19 financial year. This feeds into the preparation of revised single departmental plans, including workforce, financial and delivery plans. This ensures that departments' commitments and other essential business can be delivered with the available resource and capacity.

Departments are supported by the centre of government. The Cabinet Secretary led a series of stock-takes to examine readiness for EU Exit, to identify barriers to progress, including available capacity and capability, and actions needed to address them. Through the EU Exit Capacity and Capability Programme, the civil service takes a strategic approach to prioritising existing capacity. Examples include the targeted redeployment of members of the Fast Stream to priority EU Exit roles and the centralised resourcing of roles in priority functional areas.

The government has previously informed the Committee of its intention to publish revised SDPs in May 2018. This timescale ensures that the public versions of SDPs are directly based on departments' internal planning, which needs to be concluded first. The updated SDPs will set out how each department's activity is resourced.

Departments are prioritising their activity in different ways, and any reallocation of resource from one area to another may be partial or temporary. As a result, a binary presentation of prioritised or deprioritised work in the published SDPs is not possible. SDPs for previous years remain available when new versions are published, and can be used to monitor accountability and progress.

Notes

1 HC Committee of Public Accounts, *Managing government spending and performance*, Twenty-seventh Report of Session 2016-17, HC 710, November 2016.

2 HC Committee of Public Accounts, *Exiting the European Union*, Eighteenth Report of Session 2017–2019, HC 467, February 2018.

3 HM Treasury, *Treasury Minutes: Government responses to the Committee of Public Accounts: Sessions 2010–2012, 2012-13, 2013-14, 2014-15, 2015-16 and 2016-17* and *progress on Government Cash Management*, Cm 9566, January 2018.

4 HM Treasury, *Treasury Minutes: Government response to the Committee of Public Accounts on the Twelfth to the Nineteenth Report of Session 2017–2019*, Cm 9596, March 2018.

Source: National Audit Office

Made in United States
Cleveland, OH
04 November 2026

47506823R00045